GRANDAD'S BOOK
From Biplanes to Concorde

by

JOHN DOBSON

DEDICATION

To my wife Jeanne Dobson

CONTENTS

My Dad, John Dobson, originally wrote this book around 1992 with much encouragement from family members, especially my Mum, Jeanne Dobson.

Dad typed the manuscript using a basic typewriter having taught himself to touch type using the Pitman Typing Course. This home learning program consisted of a number of LP records with accompanying printed exercises. Basically you sat down with fingers poised over the typewriter keys, book propped open and started the record player. The music was light orchestral with a heavy metronome beat, each beat representing a keystroke. As you became more proficient you switched up to the next record with faster music until you reached 70 words per minute.

Dad persevered with the course (amidst much family hilarity) as typing would be a useful job skill to have. I can still hear the music with its relentless metronome beat and me, Mum and Roger waiting to join in with the voice on the record that would announce loudly at every pause in the music after every line of type, "Carriage Return!"

Dad had thought about producing an illustrated version using his old photographs but publishing costs were prohibitive. This book is what I think Dad would've wanted and I've used a lot of the photographs that he pasted into his master copy. It makes a fascinating read as it covers a lot of time and territory. There are also some wonderful vignettes told in Dad's laconic sense of humour.

As Dad said, after he'd splurged on a trip in Concorde, he'd flown in everything from biplanes to supersonic jets and seen changes from earth closets to flush toilets and chalk slates to computers.

He was one of what is now called "The Greatest Generation", people who lived through the depression and World War II and whose attitude was best summed up in Dad's own words, "Just get on and do it".

Anyway, I'm interrupting his narrative here and there to add comments that Dad didn't include.

Peter G. Dobson November 2012

Preface

Although it has little or nothing to do with the following narrative, the next few lines might be called a sort of preface.

My father used to tell, and this was confirmed by a cousin, about a distant forbear, how far distant was never made clear, who was coachman to a family somewhere in the Lowlands of Scotland. The story told that he eloped with the Laird's daughter and fled south, to where was not known or mentioned. However, trying to trace the family tree, I went back as far as 1820 to a baptismal entry in the church records in the village of Kirkby Overblow near Harrogate of a baby, the son of an ostler. Whether there was any tie-up between an ostler and a coachman may never be known, but as both occupations deal with horses, there may be a connection somewhere, which only further investigation may prove.

Note from Peter:
Our Dobson line can be traced back to a John Dobson who was born in the 1500s and died in Spofforth, Yorkshire in 1617. The Dobsons were all involved in farming in the area, including the villages of Dunkeswick, Kirkby Overblow and Kearby. My Dad's Grandad moved to the Darlington area around 1860. John Dobson's Father was one of nine children two of whom emigrated to form Dobson branches in New Zealand and Australia. As for the elopement with the Laird's daughter, enquiries are continuing...

This little story is written at the suggestion of a family member to write an answer to a possible question, what did you do in the war, Grandad? Then someone else suggested that I tell all about my early life, or at least as much as I can remember, of the way we used to live in those days - so different from now. It is a simple story, not meant to be a literary masterpiece, but I hope whoever reads it may find it interesting.

Chapter 1

A childhood in farming community

I was born at HIGH GRANGE,

a farm about one and a half miles from the village of Melsonby in the North Riding of Yorkshire, on the eighteenth January, 1919 at about 11.30 hours. It was Sunday and as my parents put it, I arrived just in time for dinner.

My father, Samuel Dobson, himself the son of a farm bailiff, was what was known as a farm 'hind', and we lived in a cottage on the farm. It would be a 'tied cottage' which meant that the house went with the job and was rent free.

John Dobson with parents Samuel and Margaret

Of course I have no memories of the house or farm as we left there in 1921. I went back to the farm recently and found it had a new owner who farmed the land from another farm in the area. The farmhouse had been sold just as a dwelling house in the country. The cottage had been sold too, and looked as though the new owners had extended and modernised it, again for use as a weekend cottage or country retreat if the Mercedes parked outside was anything to go by.

We left there when my father changed his job and went to work for a Mr Keenleyside who farmed at Melsonby, and this time we lived in a cottage in the village. It is an odd thing, but I can remember some events that happened then even more clearly than something that happened two days ago. I distinctly remember, in the cottage, standing on the head of a sofa we had, and falling off and gashing my head on a piece of wood on the floor in the process. I also remember having tummy ache one day, and my mother went to the pantry for the gripe water, a never failing remedy, and in the semi-darkness got hold of the wrong bottle and nearly gave me a spoonful of ammonia. It was a good job she noticed the smell in time. On another occasion, I was invited together with nearly every child in the village to the birthday party of a boy slightly older than I was, and during one game that I was too young to play in, I was put up on a table out of the way and guess what, I fell off, without hurting myself as it happened.

John Dobson aged 15 months

When I was three years old or just over, Miss Cool, the head, in fact the only teacher in the village school agreed to have me at school, mainly in the mornings, as there were no other children of my age to play with, and probably to keep me out of mischief, but I learned how to write, on a slate as we did not have any books, at a very early age. Occasionally, my aunt Jane, a widow who was also the school caretaker and lived in a cottage next door to the school looked after me after school, if my mother was out for the day. At that time there were no buses to or from the village, and travel was by bicycle, horse, pony and trap or walk, but I have a vague recollection of going to Darlington in a horse-drawn covered wagon called a 'brake' to catch a train for a day trip to Scarborough, a seaside resort on the east coast of the county. This brake was eventually replaced by a bus in 1923, I believe.

In 1924, by which time I was five years old and attending school full time, my father changed his job again, and we moved back to a farm next to High Grange, called Low Grange, which was farmed by a Mr Milner. Again we lived in a 'tied cottage' on the farm, one of a pair of cottages. It was an old house, and had no electricity, gas or water laid on. Lamps were paraffin ones and water came from a pump over a well at the back of the farmhouse a short distance away and was used by everybody on the farm. At the back of the house was the lavatory (the other cottage had its own) or earth closet or ash pit as it was called. This was a small stone building with an entrance door at the front, and inside was a wooden seat, with a hole in it to sit on. At the back was a smaller door which allowed fire ashes from the house to be thrown in to cover the debris deposited at the front. Other household rubbish was added too. Periodically, it was all cleaned out and carted away to an old quarry in one of the fields on the farm where it gradually decayed and presumably was mixed with other farmyard manure and spread on the fields in the autumn.

I do not have many memories of life on this farm, as our next door neighbours had two daughters both older than I was, consequently we did not have much in common, but a couple of things I remember well were, one winter day, some hay in a barn, two fields away from the farm buildings, caught fire and with no water handy, the farm workers, my father included, had to resort to throwing shovelfuls of snow up on to the top of the hay, but all to no avail and the hay and barn roof were burnt. The barn walls were built of stone and did not burn. My other clear memory concerns the visit of the corn thresher, a subject I will deal with more fully later, but I still remember the thresher coming to Low Grange. It was the first one I had seen at close quarters.

My most vivid memory of Low Grange was the occasion when, together with some children from a neighbouring farm, we were invited into the farmhouse (a great honour) to hear the Wireless, as it was called. This to us was the wonder of the age. It was the first one in the area and had been built by the local Rector, who apparently was genius with things temporal as well as spiritual. It was amazing, to us, to hear music and voices coming out of a funnel shaped arrangement on top of a square wooden box.

The school, of course, was much further away than it had been in the village, in fact I now had to walk one and a quarter miles across some fields and along a quiet country road to get to school, sometimes alone, and sometimes with other children from a nearby farm, so we got plenty of exercise. I recall once being a bit later than usual and was alone, the other children having gone on ahead, and was climbing the stile that led from field to road, when I saw a figure coming up the road. It was raining at the time and the figure was dressed in sacks, obviously a tramp, and I hurriedly retreated into the field and hid behind some thick bushes in the hedge. I remember being scared stiff at the time, after all I was only five.

After two years at Low Grange, my father changed his job again. This time he took a job as a horseman at a farm near Shildon in County Durham called Hawthorn Farm, which was farmed by a Mr Trotter. It was at this point that I realised that he always changed jobs in the middle of May. I also realised that a number of farm workers did likewise. Then I found out how this came about. Every year on Easter Monday, a Fair was held in Darlington and part of this fair was called 'the Wrings'. Farmers and farm workers used to congregate on the High Row and mingle with each other, i,e, farm workers wanting a change, and looking for another job, and farmers who were losing workers, looking for replacements to hire. All agreements were confirmed by a handshake, and all movements took place on or about May 13th following that Easter Monday. A simple arrangement.

Thus on May 12th. my father went to Hawthorn Farm to get a flat-topped wagon and brought it back to Low Grange. The next day all our goods and chattels and Felix, our cat were loaded on to the wagon and away we went, clippety clop to our new home, a distance of about 16 miles. We arrived safely, unloaded, and got all our furniture etc. indoors and into the proper rooms while my mother cooked a meal. Most workers moved in the hope of a better job, or more pay, or just a change. My father's latest move was all three.

As a horseman, he earned thirty five shillings a week, instead of the thirty shillings he had earned as a cowman. We had a newer and nicer house and were nearer to a town. Again we lived in a tied cottage but this one was more modern than the last two, with water laid on to a tap in the kitchen, but it was still lit by paraffin lamps. Sanitation was still an earth closet, but being near Shildon, was cleaned out more frequently by town council workmen. The only blot on the landscape on our second day there was that Felix had disappeared. At first we thought he had gone mouse hunting in the farm buildings, but when he did not reappear, we thought we had lost him. About a month later, we had a message to say that Felix was back at Low Grange. How on earth he got there, or even found his way back there was a real mystery, and still is. My father cycled over to Low Grange to collect and bring him back again, and this time we did something we had forgotten to do before, we buttered his paws. It may be considered an old wives tale, but if a cat is taken to a new home, butter its paws, and apparently it then thinks it is on to a good thing and has got a good home and will stay there. We did and he never strayed again.

In addition to being rent free, paraffin and coal were also provided free, milk and eggs were freely available from the farm sources, as were turnips and potatoes in season. Any other vegetables could be grown in the garden at the back of the house.

John Dobson's
Grandad and Grandma Race
who lived near Hamsterley, Durham

The farm was what is described as a mixed farm, some arable land, some pasture for gracing and some meadow for the hay crop. It had a dairy herd, some sheep and pigs and of course the horses, six of them. As a horseman, my father had the three horses he worked with to care for, clean and feed.

Aunt Violet at Oxmoor

With the horses he ploughed and tilled the land as necessary, cut the meadow grass in summer, cut, stocked and carted the corn into the stackyard by the farm buildings at harvest time.

Milk from the dairy herd was taken from the cow byres to the dairy, where it was put through a cooler to pasteurise it and then put into churns for the two milkmen who collected them in horse-drawn milk floats for sale in Shildon. In those days milk was sold by the milkmen carrying it in a sort of lidded bucket from house to house, and ladling it out by measuring can straight into the customer's jug. I don't think milk bottles had been invented by then, certainly not in Shildon. The cows were milked by hand, no milking machines either in those days and my mother used to help with the milking both morning and afternoon. She also kept the dairy clean, washed milk churns and milking pails, the cooler, etc and for this was paid fifteen shillings per week, so with the thirty five shillings per week, my father was paid, we were comparatively well off, compared with a lot of other workers at that time, and of course there was a lot of unemployment in the area, with men getting one pound a week dole money.

My memories of Hawthorn Farm are still fairly fresh in my mind and are quite pleasant. Our next door neighbour had a son a few months older than I was and the farmer, Mr Trotter, also had a son a little older than me, and a daughter a few months my junior. Thus we were all in the same age group and all playmates together, with plenty to occupy our time and minds on the farm. In addition to the farm animals already mentioned, there were dogs, one of them our own dog, Rover, cats and the pets of the farmer's children, a Shetland pony and a donkey, which we all played with or rode on. I remember the arrival of the donkey very well. Mr Trotter had a fairly large car, a four-door Essex super six, it was called and I even remember the number, HN 6260, and one day Mr Trotter drove off somewhere and came back about teatime complete with donkey.

The car was just wide enough to get the donkey into the space between the front and rear seats, head to one side, tail to the other. It looked so comical when it arrived. We used to spend hours trying to make it and the pony jump over a pole set on a couple of bricks on the ground, but neither of them were very enthusiastic about jumping. They would trot up to the pole, stop and step over it, and then trot on. Most disheartening.

We all went to the same school in Shildon, All Saints, less than half a mile from the farm and usually went together. One memorable occasion was seeing a total eclipse of the sun on June 29, 1927. The next one we were told, would be in 1954, which I did not see because I was overseas at the time, and the next one after that will be in 1999, I wonder if I'll see that one. We also spent a lot of time during school holidays, helping, or hindering, as children will in the fields and of course, in wet weather, in an extensive range of farm buildings and barns, games of hide and seek can go on for hours.

Another of our pastimes was watching trains and goods wagons on the railway, and taking engine numbers, a hobby which is still carried on, I believe.

The farm was situated at the top edge of a plateau which sloped fairly steeply down to a valley floor which was occupied by several acres of railway sidings and the main line from Darlington to Shildon and Weardale. Shildon had three of four coal mines in and around the town,

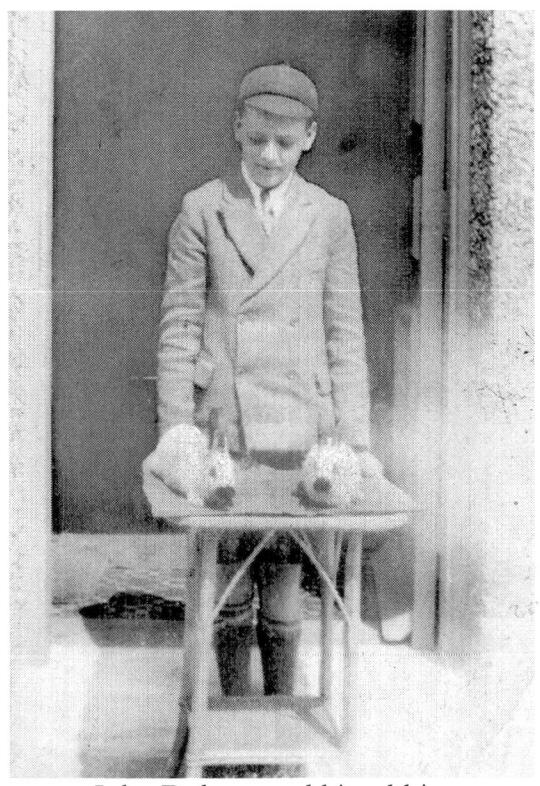

John Dobson and his rabbits

and coal was carried away on these lines, and we used to count the number of twenty-ton trucks being pulled by one engine. I forget the number now but they seemed to stretch for well over a quarter of a mile. Actually, the first passenger train ever to run in England was from Shildon to Darlington in 1825, pulled by George Stephenson's Rocket, so we were told. There used to be a plate on a post beside the railway line in Shildon giving the details. The sloping fields down towards the railway were ideal for another of our winter holiday pastimes, sledging.

Highlights in the farming calendar were of course, seasonal, Haymaking and Harvesting.

For hay, a mechanical grass cutter drawn by two horses, cut the grass and left it lying in swathes. The grass was dried by the sun, then turned over by a swathe turner for further drying, then raked into whinrows by a horse drawn rake, and the whinrows piled into haycocks or pikes (large haycocks) and then carted off to the farmyard for stacking in the haysheds, or stacked in the fields, and then thatched with wheat straw by my father who was also an expert thatcher, to keep them dry.

Corn harvesting was done by a three horse drawn machine called a binder. The corn was cut, formed into sheaves and when reaching a predetermined size, the sheaves were automatically tied with string and ejected on to the ground where they were picked up by hand and made into stocks by standing them on their bases, leaning towards each other for support, eight or ten sheaves to a stook. These after standing for two or three days for drying (providing there was no rain) were carted off to the stackyard and built up on a base of thorn hedge clippings, to allow air to get in, under the cover of a Dutch barn. If the barn was full, the corn sheaves were built up into a stack in the field and thatched like haystacks.

Later, came the threshing of the corn. At one time each farmer had his own mechanical threshing machine, but this took up a lot of space and was only used about twice or maybe three times a year. With the invention and development of the steam traction engine a mobile threshing machine could be taken to a farm, used and then on to another farm and so on. So now each farmer in turn, used to hire the services of a thresher which was brought to the farm by a steam engine. The thresher, a large, mainly wooden structure was lined up alongside the stack to be threshed, and the engine attached to it by means of an endless belt between the engine flywheel and a pulley wheel on the thresher to supply the motive power for operation. Several workers were involved in the actual work of threshing.

First, usually two men on the cornstack, forking the sheaves from the stack on to the top of the thresher, where two more people, known as band cutters stood to receive them, cut the string (band) around the sheave and pass the sheave to the feeder, a man who stood in a small pit or recess on top of the thresher behind the drum. The feeder fed the sheaves into the drum gradually and horizontally and the drum, a rapidly revolving cylinder passed the corn stalks down inside the thresher where the corn was shaken from the husks and passed over some vibrating sieves or riddles, and finally directed into chutes leading to the corn sacks attached to the end of the thresher. At the same time the corn stalks or straw was in turn passed along other riddles to the other end of the thresher, where it was formed into 'battens' which were packed again to a predetermined size, tied with string and automatically ejected. These battens were then built up into another stack for future use as animal fodder (oat straw) thatching (wheat straw) or barley straw for bedding down animals. The corn sacks, as they were filled were taken to the granary, while the chaff or husks which fell to the ground under the thresher was usually taken away, piled up and used as bedding in pig styes or for hens to scratch around in, or for burning if not needed for anything else.

After the corn harvest was completed, there were fields to be ploughed, manure to be spread on fields that needed it, stacks to be thatched, maybe, and then came the potato crop if grown.

This was usually harvested in the mid-term holiday in October, known in our area, and probably others, as 'tatie picking' holidays, when scores of school children of all ages went out from the towns and villages, on to the farms to hand pick the potato crop, for which they were paid 1/- to 2/- (shillings) a day, depending on age and ability. A horse-drawn machine known as a 'tatie scratter' went up and down the field over the rows unearthing the potatoes, which made them easy to pick up into baskets or buckets and transfer to a cart as it came along.

Many Christmas presents were bought with money earned by tatie picking no doubt. I know some of mine were. The next job was the pulling of turnips and mangolds, if grown, a very tedious job often done by gangs of Irish labourers on contract work, who in all probability had done the job of turnip hoeing in the spring. Turnips and mangolds were used for winter feeding for cows, horses, pigs, sheep, etc.

Shildon was a smallish industrial town, with a lot of people out of work even though it had three or four coal mines in or near the town. It also had a large engineering works, building or repairing railway wagons or any other sort of railway work. George Stephenson's Rocket ran from near here, as previously mentioned, at least it says so on a plate on a post close by. There were three cinemas in the town, all of which changed from 'silent films' to 'talkies' while we were there. Seats cost threepence, sixpence, ninepence or a shilling, depending on whether they were upstairs or down. One of the cinemas also staged live shows occasionally, and sometimes a pantomime at Christmas. Matinees were shown for children on Saturdays, prices twopence or fourpence depending on whether up or down.

On Sunday evenings, my parents used to go to the Soho Street Wesleyan Chapel and took me with them to the evening service. Each year the Chapel held an Anniversary Service at which the children of the congregation, and from the Sunday School used to 'sing or say a piece', in other words, sing solo, a song or hymn, or recite a piece of poetry. Having a reasonably good singing voice I became one of those who sang.

Redby House
The Pump
Samuel Dobson's
Cottage

Redworth village today

In 1928 my father decided he wanted to be his own boss, so we left Hawthorn Farm and moved to Redworth, a little village on the way to Darlington, where he became a tenant farmer, and paid rent on a small grass farm, 6 fields, part of Major Surtees estate.

There we kept a few cows, pigs and calves, some poultry and for a short while a few sheep. The house that went with the farm was actually in the village, about two hundred yards from the farm land and buildings, and it was the second largest house in the village.

What a different from the 'tied' cottages we had lived in before. It consisted of a large entrance hall with stairs up to the next floor, a big kitchen cum living room with the kitchen range in it, larder sitting room, a big scullery with a walk-in pantry from it and a large cool room with marble shelves, which we used as a dairy. Upstairs

20

there were four good sized bedrooms and a box room. Lighting was still by paraffin lamps as the village had no gas or electricity laid on, and again, water had to be carried by bucket from the village pump.

Redby House

This pump was some 50-60 yards away and was over a well fed by a spring which, we were told had never been known to go dry in living memory. It was a stone faced brick building about five feet square, with some of the stonework crumbling slightly. When we had been there three or four years, the local Council decided to dismantle the old pump and replace it with a new one. The replacement looked ghastly, it was a thin metal monstrosity with a handle down one side and a spiked cap on top. As someone said one day, it looked like a World War 1 German sentry on guard, and of course, being of thin metal, in the winter frosts, it froze up with monotonous regularity.

Behind the house was a sizeable back yard where there was a large coalhouse cum wood store, a wash house with a wash boiler in it, and next door to that was, wonder of wonders, a water closet, the only one in the village. What a change from the old ash pits. Just one snag, no handle or chain, no water. A bucket of water had to be used when required. Even so a vast improvement. Beyond the yard was a little stream with small fish in it, crossed by a plank bridge to the garden which was very useful as it contained a few fruit trees, apple, pear, plum and a lilac bush.

The Pump

There was also a patch of raspberry canes, some red and blackcurrant, and gooseberry bushes. In addition there was an area in the middle for planting potatoes and other vegetables. A short distance away, separated from our garden by another villager's garden, was our orchard, about half an acre of it just opposite the pump. Again, a number of trees, mainly apple but another plum and some flowering shrubs, plus a further area which had previously been used as a vegetable patch. We also kept some chickens in a wire enclosure in the orchard, quite secure as we thought, but one night a fox got in somehow and killed every one of them, and only took one away to eat. It is the sort of thing that foxes do. I still hate foxes.

Just a few yards away from the pump I mentioned earlier was the Wesleyan Chapel, the only place of worship in the village, where the afternoon Sunday School classes were held as well as the Sunday evening services. Again, being a Chapel, we had anniversaries which I attended and in time became quite used to singing in public. One Sunday afternoon in the summer of 1929 or 1930, I forget which, we were in Sunday School, and we became aware of the noise of engines, and being so loud, we all poured out of the Chapel on to the village green to see a most astonishing sight. The Airship R101 was cruising quite slowly over the village at a height of not much more than 1,000 feet, I should think. A most wonderful sight and one I will never forget.

Being a grass farm, we had no arable land, just pasture for grazing and meadow for hay which was processed and gathered in the same way as at Hawthorn Farm as previously explained. The main difference was that we used to borrow the necessary implements from a farmer in the village, as it wasn't worthwhile buying a horse and equipment just for three fields. The hay was stacked in the hayshed and if the shed was filled, a stack was built. I made my first stack, when I was thirteen years old, a round one and was very proud of it.

To begin with all our milk was brought down from the cow byre to the dairy where it was separated, i.e. the cream was removed by separator, and stored in the dairy, and every Wednesday, my mother used to make butter from it in a wooden end over end churn, which was made up into one pound blocks for sale to a grocery shop in Shildon. The skimmed milk after separation was either sold as such to villagers for cooking, or any other use, or fed to growing calves or pigs. The butter was taken to the shop in Shildon and groceries bought with some of the butter money.

Later, after the introduction of the MILK MARKETING BOARD by the Government, all milk went to a depot in Shildon. We had to take it down the village in churns to the bus stop, from where the bus carried them to the depot.

Village life was very pleasant, out in the country with less than twenty children in the village, boys and girls of varying ages, meant plenty of friends to play with, when not occupied on the farm. I had various kinds of pets over the years, dogs, cats, rabbits, pigeons and later I kept bees for a while. Redworth had a village green which sloped fairly steeply up from the road to a high stone wall which enclosed the grounds of Redworth Hall, the home of Major Surtees, who, I suppose would be called the Squire.

There were a lot of tall trees surrounding the Hall which formed an extensive rookery, where hundreds of rooks nested in the Spring, and a noisy lot they were too, in fact when we first moved there, I could not sleep for the first two nights because of the continuous cawing, but by the third night I had become used to it and they never bothered me again. In the late spring, a cull of young rooks was carried out by the estate gamekeeper, his two sons and anyone else who had a gun, to keep the numbers down, and to provide a meal or two for hungry people in the village, if anyone fancied one, rook pie being a very tasty dish when cooked properly. I know, we always had some.

One end of the green was flatter and level, which gave us a good place to play cricket and football on, in season. The sloping part was ideal for sledging in winter when we had snow. One of my uncles who was the village blacksmith at Norham on Tweed, made me a sledge which was the fastest in the village. Another winter pastime was skating, in a smallway. In a corner of one of our fields was a small pond fed by a spring, which when frozen over in the winter was just the thing for skating. It was only a little pond really, but it was fun and almost anything is fun when one is young.

Also in winter we had our bonfire night, 5th November, Guy Fawkes night. Combustible material was always plentiful at that time of the year as farmers usually cut their hedges back in Autumn and they gladly let us gather up the clippings and take them away for the bonfire. Some farmers who had a lot would load them on to a cart and bring them to our fire themselves. We didn't bother with a guy, just a big fire, it was a good excuse for people to get rid of their rubbish in an annual clear out.

Redworth had no school, it being only a tiny village of twenty seven houses, so all the children of school age went to Heighington C. E. School, it being the next and nearest on the way to Darlington. It was quite a nice village school with good teachers, particularly Mr Nicholson the headmaster. He was also the church choir master, and one day, after I had been there for some time, and perhaps he had heard me singing, he asked me if I would like to join the church choir. As I normally went to chapel and was a Wesleyan,

I suppose, 1 said that I would have to speak to my parents and after talking it over, they agreed and said I could, so I changed my religion, in a manner of speaking from Wesleyan to C. of E. and have remained so ever since.

I cannot see what the difference in either denomination makes if one has the same basic beliefs. I liked being in the choir as it gave me an opportunity to improve my singing ability, and I did reasonably well in it as on several occasions, and at special services I was given the chance to sing the solo part of an anthem or hymn.

One summer, during the school holidays we noticed two boys we had not seen before and discovered they were two nephews of Mrs Lightfoot, a lady who for a few years was a tenant in Redworth Hall. Major Surtees was in London or somewhere and obviously needed the money, so he rented the Hall and gardens out to the said lady and her guests. The two boys were naturally mischievous and lively as boys of thirteen or fourteen usually are and were quite daring, if not foolhardy, the way they used to ride their bikes along the top of the wall that ran along the top of the green.

The wall separating the green from the hall

The width of the wall could not have been much more than twelve inches, and if they had fallen off on the green side, it would have been a drop of at least seven feet. Although we saw them in the village occasionally, we never played with them, and they never made any overtures to us. Perhaps they didn't like to, or maybe they had been forbidden to mix with us peasants.

I got my first bike at Redworth, a small second-hand Humber which my father bought for 10/- (50p), and resold it after a year or so for the same 10/-. It was about this time that my father took over the newsagency of our local paper, the Northern Echo. Although it was in his name, I delivered the papers around the village every morning and Saturday evening and made a bit of pocket money. When I was about thirteen I needed a bigger bike, so I went to another uncle who had a cycle shop in Stockton and bought a brand-new Raleigh Roadster, all chrome plated (something new then), three speed, a really posh bike for £7. 4. 6d., a lot of money then. My father paid for it, and I repaid him eventually out of my paper money.

John Dobson and Albert Robinson

It was also about this time I had my first proper holiday. I had been away with the scouts when I was elevenish, but was not sold on the idea of joining, but this was different, all the way on my own, by bus, to

Old Buckenham in Norfolk to stay with yet another uncle, who worked as a cooper in Gaymers cider factory in Attleborough.

Uncle Ernest's house at Old Buckenham, Norfolk

At his home he had a poultry farm producing hundreds of eggs a day. I had a lovely two weeks away from home and felt quite grown up. One Saturday we went on a day trip to Yarmouth and had a most enjoyable day, particularly on the sands.

Cousin Lil and one day's egg collection

On the sands at Yarmouth with Uncle Ernest and family

In the upper classes at school, we did the usual academic subjects as well as simple science, woodwork, during which I made a beehive for future use, gardening in the school garden and beekeeping which was tied in with gardening. When the school bees swarmed I was given the swarm to go into the hive that I had made. When I left school, the hive and bees would go with me and into our garden at home.

John Dobson and his beehives

We also had lots of music and singing lessons, and each year at Christmas time, the top classes put on a concert or play in the Parish Hall. I was given the solo singing part a couple of times, also duets with a girl in the top class. In one of the plays we put on, Ghosts and Ethereals, by an author whose name I have forgotten, I played Professor Bookworm in the leading role.

I consider that for a small village school, 1 received quite a good general education. The usual subjects were well taught, and even though I seemed to do reasonably well in class and end of term exams, I did not pass what in those days was called the scholarship exam, or as it became known later, the eleven plus. But I cannot have been all that thick because later in life when I was over 50 I got 5 good 'O' Levels.

Note from Peter:
Dad was highly intelligent and often said, without boasting, that he was one of the brightest at the school. He found out later that village politics had come into play as the two kids that had passed the scholarship to higher education, were not only the "thickest" of their class also happened to be the sons of prominent and wealthy parents.

Not long after this, having on the whole enjoyed them, my schooldays came to an end and I left school at Easter 1933 aged fourteen years.

I had a couple of small jobs in Darlington, mainly for pocket money, although one lasted a few months until a minor mishap on my bicycle caused me to give it up, and as there was insufficient work on the farm to keep two of us fully occupied, a shortage of suitable jobs in the vicinity made me decide to leave home and seek work further afield. Meanwhile I had sold my beehives and part-exchanged my bike for a Raleigh Racer soon after I left school.

Chapter 2

To London and Below Stairs

Owing to the difficulty and cost of getting accommodation away from home, I decided, as a friend had already done, to go into 'service'. I applied for and got a job as a 'Hall Boy' at 92 Eaton Square, in London, the home of a bachelor gentleman called Mr Ivor Ferguson. He was obviously a very rich man, elderly, white haired, and lived alone with a staff of thirteen servants, eleven in the house and two in the mews. A way of life that changed with the coming of World War 2 and never returned afterwards, and probably never will. Still, it was a job and like a horse on a good farm, I was fed and watered regularly and bedded down comfortably at night.

Eaton Square was just that, a large oblong really, of massive town houses, with enclosed and gated gardens in the middle where the occupiers or their servants could exercise their dogs safely. It was bisected in the middle by Kings Road running through the centre from Grosvenor Place to Sloan Square, with Belgrave Place running across it the other way.   It was an area where the rich and famous, and mostly titled lived in houses, each with a staff of servants, depending on the status and wealth of the owner. The whole area, I believe, belonged to the Duchy of Westminster and each house would be on long lease to the family who occupied it.

No. 92 was one such house, in a terrace with an imposing frontage, and consisted of a basement (below street level) where male servants were accommodated. The kitchen and scullery, butler's pantry, valet's room, housekeeper's room, footmen's room and servants' hall were also in this area. At this same level, but outside the house and under the pavement were toilets and a bathroom, coal and coke cellars. The next floor up from the basement was for family occupation, a magnificent hall with a marble floor, a dining room, a drawing room leading to a sun lounge at the back of the house, and above those, the bedrooms etc. The top floor was taken up with female staff quarters, i.e. housemaids, cook and kitchen staff.

92 Eaton Square, London

The indoor staff consisted of, in order of seniority and importance, the butler, the valet, the cook, two footmen, three housemaids, kitchen maid, scullery maid and the hall boy, me. At the back of the house, in the mews, was a garage, housing the car, a coach house for the brougham, stabling for the horse, and over all these accommodation for the coachman and chauffeur.

The whole house was centrally heated by radiators fed from a huge boiler in the kitchen. There were also fireplaces in the family rooms, but they were rarely used. I think they were there more for decoration than anything else, beautiful to look at but mainly remains of an age before radiators were invented.

Whenever Mr Ferguson left the house to go visiting, he went by car or brougham, and on any of these excursions, he was accompanied by a footman as well as the chauffeur or coachman. On these occasions, both the chauffeur or coachman and the accompanying footman had to be properly dressed for the drive in accordance with the prevailing weather conditions. By car, a huge royal blue, open fronted Rolls Royce with his coat-of-arms emblazoned on the doors, in cold weather both men wore a long thick heavy overcoat, a long white rubberised mackintosh was worn, with a peaked cap of course. If the trip was by brougham, both men wore the same type of clothing, but instead of a peaked cap, each man wore a top hat with a cockade on the side of it. These outfits and others I shall mention later were all made to measure and must have cost a small fortune.

For normal indoor wear, there was a strict code of dress for mornings and evenings. The butler's dress in the mornings was, black pin-striped trousers, a white shirt, black tie and a short black jacket. Evening wear consisted of black trousers, a black tail coat and black bow tie. The footmen, in the morning wore black trousers, a black tie and a black and yellow striped waistcoat. Evening wear was the same but also included a royal blue tail coat with a black bow tie.

When a dinner party was being held in the house, things were different. The butler wore black knee breeches, black stockings and black buckled shoes, a black tail coat and a white bow tie. Footmen wore yellow knee breeches, white stockings, black buckled shoes, a yellow waistcoat, a blue tail coat with gold aiguilettes, a black bow tie and powdered hair. If the dinner party was fairly large, the valet was called in to assist and he wore the same as the butler, but with a black bow tie. The footmen dressed their hair by washing it, leaving the soap suds on, then liberally applying talcum powder. Another point about the butler and footmen, they had to be at least six feet tall, and all the uniforms etc were made by Simpsons of Audley Street, for each person. When I arrived there one of the first things I had to do was to go to Simpsons and be measured for a hand made suit for wear in the afternoons and evening, even though I was not concerned with work above stairs. The suit was a lovely charcoal grey worsted material and fitted me like a glove.

All the staff had their own respective duties: the valet was responsible for Mr Ferguson's well being and his wardrobe and occasionally assisting in the dining room when required.

The butler was the boss man below stairs.

Mr. Wiseman the Butler and a kitchen maid

He had his own room in the basement and was in complete charge of the two footmen and myself. He was also in charge of the butler's pantry which had a large walk-in safe where all the silver, china tea and dinner services, and glassware was kept stored. He also held the key to the wine cellar. The two footmen also shared a room in the basement which they looked after themselves. Their duties were more or less self explanatory. They waited at table, answered the door to callers, attended the fires upstairs on the rare occasions they were needed, carefully washed china and glass after meals, cleaned silver, accompanied Mr Ferguson on his outings, and I suppose, were training themselves for a post as a butler one day.

My duties were comparatively simple: do as I was told, and one day I might be a footman or even a butler. But as things stood at the moment, I did as I was told and was responsible for such things as keeping the toilet and bathroom in the basement clean, scrubbing by hand, the basement passage once a week, attending to the kitchen boiler which heated all the water in the house (first thing in the morning, open the damper, rake out the clinker, fill with coke, maintain during the day in winter, top up at night and partly close the damper. In summer the damper was partly closed during the day). I also had to keep the servants hall clean, collect food from the kitchen, take it to the servants hall and serve the staff, hence the term 'hall boy'. The senior staff ate in the housekeeper's room and I had to take food from the kitchen and serve them. I slept in the servants' hall in a bed which folded up into a cupboard after use. The kitchen staff were responsible for the preparation and cooking of meals for the whole household indoors and we ate very well, plenty of food and well cooked.

The house maids were concerned with the cleaning etc of all rooms above the basement, and the butler's and housekeeper's rooms in the basement. The valet looked after his own, himself.

On dinner party nights, after I had been there a few months, I was allowed to carefully wash dinner plates, glassware and silver in the butler's pantry as part of my training. I was shown the proper way to clean silver. Some could be, and was cleaned with plate polish, but the best silver was cleaned and polished with rouge and finger and thumb. Thus the training was thorough,

One of Mr Ferguson's customs, and apparently he did this every year, was to give each member of staff two tickets for any theatre they would like to visit. Chose the theatre and chose the show, the butler obtained the tickets, and then we were invited up into the inner sanctum, as it were, and Mr Ferguson gave us the tickets personally. A nice little touch I thought. As it was my first visit to a London theatre, I chose the show 'JILL DARLING' at the Saville theatre with Jessie Mathews in the leading role. Not knowing many people in London, I took as my partner, a young parlour maid I knew slightly from a house in Chesham Street, near Eaton Square. We had a lovely time and thoroughly enjoyed the experience, as it was the first time for both of us.

John Dobson at the entrance of 92 Eaton Square

Unlike many of his contempories, Mr Ferguson did not have a country house or estate, so each summer he would rent one, and the year that I was there he rented one in Hampshire. It was called Rotherwick Hall, not far from Basingstoke, and was, I believe the home of the Cayzer family, something to do with shipping I think. The owners were abroad for the summer on their holidays and everyone from Eaton Square, except the housemaids, who remained in London to give 92 a thorough spring clean, were transported to Rotherwick by train and bus for a seven week break. That year the summer was particularly fine and sunny and we had a very pleasant time in the extensive and beautiful gardens, and the surrounding countryside, and I did quite a bit of exploring on my bike. I found my way up on to the roof of the Hall one day and discovered some flat places to sunbathe on when the sun came out and stayed out.

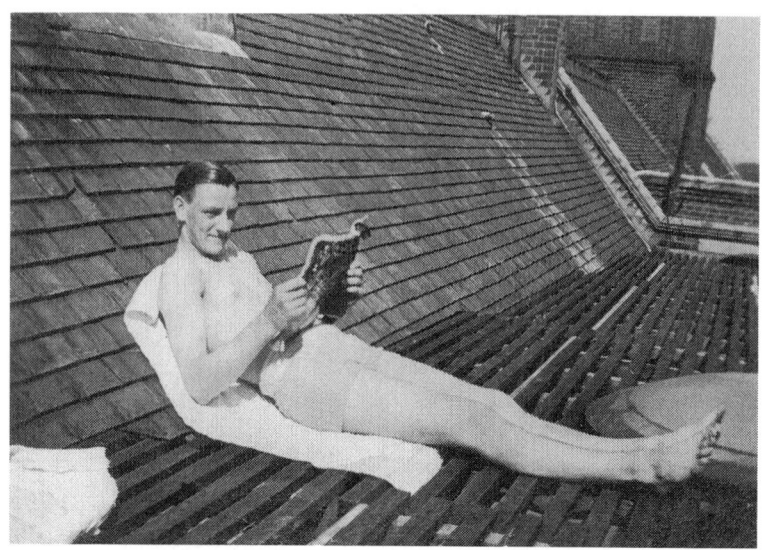

On the roof at Rotherwick Hall 1934

Actually I was rather glad to get away from London for a while. The previous Easter my mother became very ill suddenly, and although I had hurried home as quickly as I could, she had died before I got there, which shook me up quite a lot. After the funeral was over and the house settled down again, I went back to London to get over it.

This time I took my bike with me on the train and it turned out to be a godsend on my afternoons off, which were fairly frequent, and on my one half-day a week off, I enjoyed riding round London and exploring places, especially the parks, something one couldn't do nowadays at all.

During that summer at Rotherwick, what with exploring, on the roof sunbathing, chatting to the villagers one met, time seemed to fly by and almost before we knew it, we were back in London again. Autumn crept up on us and soon winter was approaching fast.

I cannot recall why, but I started to get itchy feet, perhaps the summer in the country had unsettled me. Although my salary of £30 per annum, with all food seemed fairly adequate, I began to think of pastures new as it would probably be at least two years before I could hope to get a job as a footman. Plus the fact that I wasn't completely sure that I wanted one. So I started to look around for another job, preferably one where I could get accommodation easily and cheaply. Then I found the very thing, to work in a shop, Sainsburys the grocers, where the hours would be more regular and maybe a bit shorter in numbers. I had been told that some, if not all, Sainsburys shops in London and the Southern Counties (they were a large company, even then) had flats above them where members of the staff who lived away from the area could live, and this accommodation was subsidised by the firm. A housekeeper and one or more housemaids were employed in these flats by the company to feed and look after the shop staff who lived in them.

After a little, but not too much thought I decided to change my occupation. Having been interviewed and offered a job with Sainsburys, I was spared the bother of having to give notice of my intention to leave Eaton Square by reason of a slight disagreement I had with the valet, who falsely accused me of doing something I did not do, and after he inferred that I was a liar, I clouted him. A very silly thing to do really, but nobody calls me a liar, when I'm not, and gets away with it. But it meant that I couldn't stay there any longer, and I left a little sooner than I had intended.

After leaving 92, sadly in some ways, I headed for the Holloway Road branch in North London where newcomers to the firm were billeted while they were on a three week induction course at the firm's Headquarters at Blackfriars. I arrived a few days earlier than expected, but there was plenty of room and they didn't mind so there was no problem, and I started my course the following Monday morning with several other new entrants.

The course was quite interesting and dealt with matter new to me. We breakfasted at Holloway, caught a bus or the tube train to Blackfriars, and during the day were instructed in the mysteries of the grocery trade. We were told what to do in shops and how to do it, given information about the various commodities sold and spent a lot of time learning how to weigh and serve the various types of butter, lard and margarines. We were also shown the correct way to pluck and dress poultry, especially chickens and turkeys, and the way to 'bone' a side of bacon, and how to carve a York ham, one of Sainsburys specialities. These latter things of course, we would learn more about when we got to the shop we would work in, and reached that stage in our careers. We had lunch in the Headquarters canteen, and our evening meal at Holloway Road. On the successful completion of the course, we were told which shop we would be going to, and I was sent to the Church Street, Enfield, Branch.

There I lived with two other chaps above the shop with an elderly housemaid and housekeeper to cater for our needs. We each had our own room, so we were quite comfortable and the food was more than adequate and well cooked. My biggest regret in my whole life was that I allowed myself to be encouraged to start smoking cigarettes by one of my colleagues there.

I admit now that it is a pernicious habit and a complete waste of money, when I think of what I must have spent before I managed to give it up when I was 40 years of age and my health has been much better ever since.

As a junior in the shop, naturally I had to start at the bottom of the ladder, on eggs and poultry. The double-fronted shop was recessed back at the front for about three feet, and each morning at eight o'clock (opening time in those days) I first of all had to clean the shop windows, and then set up a couple of low tables, one at each side of the shop doorway, one to stand the boxes of eggs on, and at the other side, put out a display of already dressed chickens, ducks etc and at Christmas time of course, turkeys and a few game birds, and while this was being done, even serve the odd early customer.

I had to stand there all day selling produce with the odd break for refreshment, a meal or call of nature. I must say that I enjoyed it to begin with, met and got to know many people, some of them as regular customers, especially one nice old lady who used to come along every Saturday evening, just before closing time to buy any cracked eggs that were available and were cheaper than undamaged ones. I think perhaps she took in lodgers and money was a bit tight. I used to keep half a dozen or so for her and if, when she came, I hadn't got half a dozen, and the manager wasn't watching, I used to gently crack a couple and pop them into a bag.

We were open till 6.00pm on Monday and Tuesday, half day closing on Wednesday, 6.00pm on Thursday, 8.00pm on Friday and on Saturday we were open until 9.00pm. Sundays we were free of course, and two or three of us younger ones used to cycle all over North London and the surrounding districts. Sometimes in summer, if fine, we used to go as far as Southend, and once I went to visit an uncle who lived at Hitchin. I joined the local Y.M.C.A. amateur boxing club but did not like having my nose made to bleed every time someone hit it, so packed up boxing and started playing table tennis, billiards and snooker in the same club, but was not very good at any of those either.

After a few months on 'eggs', a new boy came to the shop and took over my job and I moved inside the shop, up the next step of the ladder on to the butter counter. Several types of butter, salted and unsalted, some margarine and some lard all came to the shop in bulk initially, and were divided roughly into pounds and half pounds in the cellar by drawing a taut wire through the block of butter etc and brought up into the shop on a tray. Then as customers stated their requirements, the butter or whatever, was removed from the block and put on the scales. If under or over weight, butter was added or removed to obtain the correct weight. This was done by means of two hand-held 'butter pats', a light, thin, broad bladed cutter and a heavier, thicker wooden shaper, grooved on the underside to give it grip. Difficult to describe without a diagram.

These actions were carried out on a large flat slate bed with a raised front cover. Once weighed and shaped, the butter was transferred to paper and wrapped. Written down, it sounds a long and complicated operation, but once one got the hang of it, it was done in seconds, and this we had learned to do on the training course.

Accuracy was most important as we could be visited at any time and without warning by head office 'buyers' coming to the shop to test, and woe betide any assistant giving the wrong weight. Money went into an open till, no cash registers in those days and no till receipts. Most women knew to a penny how much they had spent, and how much change was required.

Sainsburys shops were divided into sections, each one selling different commodities, and assistants went from one counter to another to gain experience and knowledge of the whole grocery trade, e.g. eggs and poultry, butter etc, cheese and bacon, delicatessen and pork and lamb, in that order. General dry goods and deliveries were usually dealt with by girls at another counter. Some of the larger branches had a full butchery service.

Starting at my age, an assistant would receive a pay rise after six months service, a further one after twelve months and then an annual rise after each year of service till he or she reached the age of 21. At this point the assistant should have spent some time in all sections and if considered competent, was given red buttons to wear in his white jacket instead of black ones. This was a sign of ability and seniority and at this stage his salary would be £4 a week which was quite good then, even in London. Thereafter, an annual increase of 4/-per week was paid, but I do not know what the maximum that could be earned was. Unfortunately I never reached those dizzy heights.

Each Christmas, the poultry trade increased enormously and much was made of fresh birds especially turkeys. They started coming into the shops about five days before Christmas, gutted but not plucked and dressed, and every evening, as soon as the shop closed, everyone except the girls started plucking and dressing birds, and this went on until about 4.00 - 4.30 in the morning, then a few hours sleep and back to normal work. By 4.00 on Christmas Eve, everyone was shattered and needed the Christmas holiday to recover. The only good thing was that everybody involved received a full extra week's pay in recompense as overtime was not normally paid for.

My second Christmas there, I was given permission to leave work early as I did not feel well. I caught a train from Kings Cross to Darlington, arriving there about 6.00am Christmas morning. My father had left a bike for me at the station the night before and I rode home to Redworth, getting in about 7.00 o'clock. I went straight to bed and did not wake up until teatime on Boxing Day. I had flu and could not go back to work till New Year's Day.

The following February I was transferred to a new branch in Leicester, where instead of living above the shop, I lived in digs a short walk from the shop, with several other members of the staff.

Being nearer home I could visit my father more easily, and one weekend I was at home seeing him, now living in a cottage in the village, as he had given up the farm after my mother died.

While I was there, I was in Heighington one day where I met an old school friend, home on leave, in Royal Air Force Uniform. I took one look at my friend in blue and thought 'Cor! I like that, that's for me, and after returning to Leicester, I thought about it for a week or two, made my mind up and applied to join the R. A. F. My application was accepted, and I left my job, my digs, my friends in Leicester and Leicester itself and went off as directed to the recruiting centre in Birmingham. There I was given a railway travel warrant, the first of many to come, to take me to R. A. F. West Drayton in West London where I actually joined the ROYAL AIR FORCE.

On 5th May 1937, aged 18, I was sworn in and became:

540416 A.C. 2   DOBSON J.

Chapter 3

The R.A.F.

Next day, a whole crowd of us who had just joined were taken to R.A.F. Uxbridge for recruit training. There, 144 young men, all bright eyed and bushy tailed, as the saying goes, formed a Flight consisting of 6 squads of 24 men in each. We were accommodated in Kut barrack block, 24 men in each of 6 rooms with a corporal P. T. I. (Physical Training Instructor) in charge of each room. Our Cpl was a Cpl Fusedale, who, we were told, but not by him, had been the R. A. F. Welterweight Champion boxer for a few years - obviously not a man to be trifled with. Actually he turned out to be a great bloke. So our instructor was a very fit man and he proceeded to make sure that at the end of our sixteen week course, we would be fit too. We were to be with him for the full 16 weeks square bashing, as it was called, for foot drill, arms drill, how to march properly and how to salute and Officer, physical training etc, but before all this there were certain formalities to be gone through.

Before starting our actual training, we all had to have a medical and dental inspection. We were vaccinated against smallpox, given injections against tetanus, tuberculosis, and typhoid, and having had all that lot, providing we were fit enough, we then went to the stores to be issued with uniform and equipment. At one time RAF personnel wore 'dog collared' tunics, breeches and puttees, boots and peaked caps for walking out, and trousers for working. Our flight was the last one to be issued with this uniform. The next flight and all subsequent ones would be given an open-necked tunic and slacks for walking out, and keep the same working dress as before.

The remainder of our kit and equipment was the same, and the following is a list of what we were given: Boots, gym shoes, socks, 3 shirts and collars, underwear, 3 towels, 2 pairs pyjamas, 1 pair woollen gloves, a woollen long sleeved pullover, a greatcoat, brushes for clothes, buttons and boots and shaving and hair, (electric razors hadn't been invented then) a 'button stick', a 'hold all' to keep ones knife, fork and spoon in, a ration bag, a 'housewife' - a small pouch containing needles and thread and some blue darning wool, a forage cap for work and a peaked cap for parades and walking out.

R.A.F. Uxbridge 1937

Then came the webbing equipment: an upper and lower rucksack, a haversack and strap, ammunition pouches, a rifle sling, a bayonet frog, a ceremonial belt, a water bottle and carrier, a set of straps to fasten all this lot together, and finally, a large canvas kitbag to carry it around in. I nearly forgot, we were also issued with an anti-gas cape (which also did duty as a groundsheet) and a gas mask. Later we were to be issued with a 'tin hat' and a woollen cap comforter to wear underneath it, a most useful item which I still have and use to cover my scanty locks on cold days in the garden. I cannot think of anything else, but I may have missed something. All that gear was quite a load to cart around the country with me.

I quite enjoyed the training and P.T. that we were put through and became a very fit man for probably the first time in my life, and I didn't really mind doing the odd guard duty that we had to do, or even the cookhouse fatigues, potato peeling, or testing our gas masks in the gas chamber. It was all part of the system.

One of my main memories of my time at Uxbridge was being a member of a flight which took part in the annual, but sadly, the last Hendon Air Display. This was an exhibition at Hendon Aerodrome in North London (now an area of houses and factories), of all sorts and makes of aircraft, and equipment, and display of flying skills, and had been for some years the highlight of the R.A.F. year. Part of the airfield is now the home of the Royal Air Force Museum.

Our flight were all dressed up in 'uniforms' that had been used in some film with a lot of pirates etc in it and had been resurrected from some film studio. In the middle of the airfield a canvas and wooden framework of a fort had been erected and we, as pirates were attacking it while being bombed by Hawker Hinds, supposedly bombing us. Strategically placed smoke bombs and fireworks made a realistic display of a bombing attack and we were bombed out of existence while the fort and its defenders remained intact.

John Dobson on right with Hawker Hind

One of the last things we did before we finished our training was to be taught how to start an aircraft engine by 'swinging the prop'. This was the method used when other means were not available. It needed a crew of four people, the pilot or perhaps engine fitter in the cockpit to operate the switches and three men on the propeller to do the donkey work, and we were shown how, on a wingless fuselage in a building on the camp. The three men lined up in front of the aircraft, No 1 facing the engine and holding the propeller, No 2 had his back to the engine and held No 1's hand, No 3 faced the engine and held No 2's free hand. The engine was primed and at the given signal, all three men ran sideways with No 1 pulling the propeller round. As they did so the man in the cockpit operated the starting switch and the engine fired and started, if not, repeat and repeat again, and again the procedure until it did. The idea of three men was for safety. As the engine fired the propeller whipped round and if number one had not been pulled away, he might have been hit by the propeller with disastrous results, but by having two men pulling, he was pulled clear.

LAST OF THE SWINGERS - Wapiti in oil by Douglas Swallow

The picture gives a better view of the operation perhaps than my explanation. Nowadays that method is rarely used as jet engines have internal batteries or external starting devices and engine starting is much easier, and more certain.

Then in September 1937, after completing our initial training, I was posted to R.A.F. Dishforth in the North Riding of Yorkshire, on to my first squadron, No 10 Bomber Squadron where, for a while I was employed in the flight office of 'B' flight. My flight sergeant was called Mitchell. He was an old timer, wearing World War 1 campaign medal ribbons and his service number was 2337. His contemporary in 'A' flight was called Pynne, I think and his number was 2339 and it seemed that after every telephone call between them, they exhorted each other to 'get some in'. I always used to think, both had already got some in'.' The squadron was equipped with Whitleys, a new heavy bomber, replacing the old biplane Heyford, one of which the sqdn, still had in the hanger, but unserviceable.

Dishforth was a new station, with the airfield bordering the Great North Road (now the A.I) and was one of the new expansion scheme airfields as they were called. In 1935-36 the international situation called for a rapid increase in the armed forces, especially the R.A.F. and airfield construction was taking place all over the country, Dishforth being one of them. Leeming a few miles to the north was another, and Linton-on-Ouse yet another, a few miles to the south, and that was only the Vale of York.

No barrack blocks had been built yet and we lived in wooden huts, 24 men to a hut with a corporal's bunk at the end of it, and a store room opposite. Most other buildings were also of wooden construction, as were the messes, Naafi, sick quarters, Education section/Church and guardroom. In fact the only permanent buildings when I arrived were the Armoury, four hangers and the Airmens married quarters. Building was going on everywhere though. The huts were in two lines, one for each sqdn (78 Sqdn was our sister Sqdn there), and a few more for the staff of headquarters. Between the two lines were the ablution huts and toilets. The floors in the huts were just bare boards, which had to be scrubbed every friday afternoon. Heating came from two coal/coke stoves, one at each end. Each man had a bed, a bedside locker, a shelf on the wall above the bed head, and a wooden kit box which went under the bed, no luxuries at all.

I started to play hockey while I was there, rather badly at first, but I improved as the season went on and became a member of the station team, playing other teams, Service and civilian in the area on Wednesday and Saturday afternoons and now and again on Sunday mornings.

On one occasion I was detailed as a member of a crash guard, four men and a Cpl. on a Whitley that had crash-landed in a field just outside York, shortage of fuel it was said.

Another time I had been to Thirsk on my bike and was riding back to camp in brilliant moonlight and no bike lamp, when suddenly a large policeman jumped from by a hedge and stopped me for riding without a light. I agreed I had no light but in the moonlight and no traffic about, I didn't think it was dangerous, politely of course, besides it was getting near the time when I should be back in camp, 21.30 hours. After giving me a 'ticking-off, I was allowed to go on my way, providing I walked an pushed the bike. Off I went plodding along the side of the road, he got on his bicycle and went off towards Thirsk. I saw him out of sight, and thought, oh hell! I'm going to be late, so mounted the bike to ride on again, while he must have known of a short cut and guessed what I would do, and sure enough, at the next road end, there he was again. No messing about this time, number, rank and name? I would be reported, he said and then he rode off. I walked a few yards and then thought, in for a penny, in for a pound, I'll be late anyway, so mounted and rode off reaching the guardroom safely and just in time.

It was a few months later, when I was on another station, that a letter caught up with me and said I was to appear in court on such and such a day. There was no way I could do that, so I had to write and admit to my heinous crime, say I was sorry and it would not happen again, and about a month after that, I had another letter to say I had been found guilty and find 4/- (20p), pay up and look happy.

A much more pleasant memory and experience, was my first flight in an aeroplane, a Whitley. This was as a passenger on a five and a half hour night navigation trip round England. As it was my first trip, it was a lovely occasion, but cold. I was sitting in an empty space right at the back of the fuselage, where later, a gun turret would be fitted. I could see quite clearly through a perspex panel in the end skin and looking backwards as we flew through the darkness, and saw the lights of the villages and towns looking like fairy lights as we flew over them about 6,000 feet up is something I will never forget.

Armstrong Whitley

As a result of this trip I got the bug for flying and applied to become a spare-time air gunner which would have meant more pay, 1s/6d a day, but alas I failed the medical exam, through not having sufficiently good eyesight, a must for an air gunner. To be honest now in retrospect, I'm glad, as I believe, that of all the other chaps who were spare-time A.G.'s at that time, only ten per cent survived the war.

Another pleasant recollection is of something that happened fairly frequently, walking down to Boroughbridge from camp at night, about one and a half miles, to Kelly's cafe for a mixed grill. A huge plateful that had everything in it, bacon, sausage, chop, egg, beans, tomatoes, mushrooms and anything else you can think of with tea and bread and butter, all for 1s/6d old money, 7 1/2p now, and then walk back to camp. When staying on camp we spent a lot of time playing cards, snap, pontoon, solo whist etc for pennies, so we never won or lost very much.

Occasionally I cycled over to Ripon for a pint, or being nearer home, if not playing hockey I was able to get home to Redworth by train and bus for the weekend. Then needing to earn more pay, I decided to be trained for a trade, and at the end of the hockey season, I was posted to R.A.F. Eastchurch on the Isle of Sheppey in Kent for training as an armourer at No 1 Armament School.

Eastchurch camp was situated just outside the village of the same name and was about six miles from Sheerness. We were housed in the usual wooden huts even though it was an old camp, 24 men to a hut, the usual two heating stoves, two tables, two forms, but the floor was covered with brown linoleum, which had to be polished once a week, normally on a Friday night ready for Saturday morning inspection. I managed to get a few games of hockey during the season, but only on Wednesday afternoons, the official sports day. Went to the village pub, The Crooked Billet, fairly frequently for a pint and a game of darts. Saturday nights, some of us usually went to Sheerness to a dance or the cinema.

Caught by a street photographer on Sheerness sea front

A friend of mine had a motor bike so transport was no problem. During early summer in 1938 I spent some pleasant hours at the weekends on the grass and gorse covered cliffs close to Leysdown, it was a beautiful sunbathing spot.

Dad's tale here, of travelling on the back of his friend's motorbike through a country lane on very dark night when they saw a stranded motorcyclist working on the bike at the side of the road. Naturally they stopped to offer assistance and found that the bike was a very old model and the motorcyclist, who was all covered in leather suit and helmet, indicated that the trouble was the headlight, an old carbide one. These worked on the principal of dripping water from a reservoir onto calcium carbide to produce acetylene gas which was lit and burned very brightly. My Dad's outgoing friend spotted that the reservoir was empty and anxious to help and show off his knowledge, simply unbuttoned his fly and peed in it, a traditional method of supplying water to the reservoir in an emergency. Problem solved and with headlight working the motorcyclist headed off with a wave of thanks miming agreement to buy them a pint at the next pub. Dad and friend followed after, wondering why the owner of a vintage motorbike wasn't aware of the quick headlight fix. The answer became clear when they met the motorcyclist at the pub. Standing at the bar waiting for them was a good looking blonde female in leathers and a big smile who thanked Dad's embarrassed friend for his help and said that she just didn't have the right 'equipment' to refill the reservoir that way.

One problem we did have in September 1938 was when at one point war with Germany seemed imminent, and we were taken from our classrooms down to the playing fields, where we spent two or three days digging trenches for use as air raid shelters in the event of being bombed, if war did come. Fortunately, the threat of war receded and we resumed our studies.

Eventually, end of course exams were taken and I only achieved 59% which meant that I became an A. C. 2 Armourer. I should have done better, even only 60% would have made me an A. C. 1 and consequently more pay, but I guess I spent too much time in the Crooked Billet, and not enough time on my books. The chap in the bed across the room from me was a bit of a swotter and rarely went out and he got 80% and became an L. A. C., the only one on the course. There must be a moral there somewhere.

Then in October 1938 my posting after the course was to 40 Squadron at R.A.F. Abingdon as an armourer. The Sqdn operated single engined light bombers, Fairey Battles. Abingdon too, was an older station and we were accommodated in brick built barrack blocks, again 24 men to a room, but still heated by two coal/coke stoves and floors covered with lino which had to be kept polished. Being a permanent one, the whole station was brick built, including Messes and N.A.A.F.I. The nearest town, as one would expect, was Abingdon, a smallish place on first impressions, and seemed to consist principally of one long main street which was said to contain 57 pubs and to be considered to have 'arrived' and be 'in' on the station, one was supposed to drink a pint of beer in every one of them in a week. Needless to say I could not afford it, not even in half pints, but I tried. Being fairly close to Oxford, and as I managed to get into the station hockey team, I played in a few games against college teams at the University and was enjoying being at Abingdon, but my joy was short lived and my stay there equally short, and I was on my way again, this time in February 1939 to R.A.F. Cottesmore near Oakham in the county of Rutland.

Cottesmore was another expansion scheme airfield, but a little later in being started than the other ones I had been on. Again, like Abingdon, there were two squadrons of Fairey Battles, 35 and 207.

My posting was to 35 Sqdn and on arrival, I found five or six other armourers who had been on the same course at Eastchurch as I had and who had been posted elsewhere originally and now, like me, re-posted to Cottesmore, some to 35 and some to 207, so at least I was among friends. We were told that we had been posted in to bring the squadrons up to full strength in readiness for a move overseas to the Far East, which meant either Singapore or Hong Kong. As it transpired however, the move was cancelled and we stayed at Cottesmore, which was a little disappointing in a way, but as things turned out later, maybe a blessing.

Attending to a crash landing in the snow at Cottesmore

There we were back in wooden huts again and as the station was in the very early stages of construction, there was mud all over the place. Luckily as the year went into spring and early summer, it dried up quite a bit. There was no likelihood of any hockey there for some time as no sports field had been laid out yet. However, it was beautiful countryside around in the heart of rural England with several small towns all within easy reach, Oakham the county town, Melton Mowbray, Grantham and Stamford handily placed for visiting. I had another flight while I was there, this time in an Avro Anson, a twin engined light bomber and trainer up to Evanton in Scotland, stayed overnight and returned next day.

On the way there we passed over my home village, Redworth at a height of around 2,000 feet and looking down I could see my sister hanging washing out to dry in the garden. From that height I couldn't actually recognise her, but I knew the position of the garden in the village, there was no mistaking it. Little did she know that I was watching her from above. On the way back it was cloudy, and I do not know what our actual route was.

Later I had another trip in a Fairey Battle, this time sitting in the Air Gunner's seat at the back. During my time at Cottesmore I sat and passed the exam for A.C.1 and was reclassified as such. Cottesmore was to be my last peacetime posting, as towards the end of August, part of the squadron went to hold a two-week practice camp at Catfoss on the East Yorkshire coast not far from Hornsea. This meant sending six aircraft together with all the necessary ground staff and

equipment, and aircrew for practice bombing and gunnery on land and sea targets
. All went well the first week, but on Sunday, September 3rd, war was declared and we all packed up immediately and returned to Cottesmore.

After a few days to pack all our kit and equipment, both personal and squadron, the whole squadron and 207 moved en bloc to Cranfield in Bedfordshire, to become a training squadron, in other words, some of our aircrew were posted to operational squadrons and new recruits were sent to us to be trained to operational standard.

Chapter 4

Wartime

My memories of Cranfield are rather vague, we were working all sorts of hours, and initially were confined to camp till the first panic died down, then we were allowed out for three hours at a time only, if we went out at 6.00pm we had to be back by 9.00pm and so on. Gradually however, the situation eased, and we became more organised and were able to have more free time and could get out into the neighbouring small towns and villages for longer periods than three hours, time to have a couple of beers, but we still worked seven days a week, and forty eight hour passes were a thing of the past. It was at Cranfield where I was reclassified L. A. C. (Leading Aircraftsman) quite a milestone in my short career.

Then early in December 1939, both squadrons were mobile once more. This time to Bassingbourn, not far from Cambridge, again a completely new airfield of the same name, still in the process of construction, but a little more advanced in some things, than some we had been on. We actually moved into a barrack block so new, it had not been furnished properly, and for the first night there, in lieu of mattresses, we each had to fill a palliasse with straw from a heap in the corner of the room. There were no wall cupboards or bedside lockers, only wooden kit boxes which went under the bed, no heating except two small paraffin stoves, but at least there were blankets, no sheets but the wash rooms had hot water. It was nearly a week before we got proper mattresses and also by that time there was actually central heating on. Goodbye coke and paraffin stoves. As usual there was mud all over the place, except where the snow had not melted, on the roads. Where there were no roads, it was just mud under the snow. As days passed, things gradually improved and a change in the weather allowed flying to be resumed, until it snowed again. In our off duty periods we could get into Cambridge by bus, but owing to the black-out, it was not very pleasant after dark.

Christmas came and went almost un-noticed. I say almost, but I've just remembered that on Christmas Eve, I had been with friends to a party and, as at parties when one is enjoying oneself, I didn't notice the passage of time and suddenly realised the last bus had gone. Taxis were not available, so when the party was over, I slept fitfully on a sofa

*With Permission to Wear Plain Clothes............
*Delete if not applicable.   (Initials).

ROYAL AIR FORCE.

Station ....CRANFIELD....
Unit.... No. 85 Squadron.
No. 540416 Rank L.A.C. #
Name.... DOBSON T

has permission to be absent from
his Quarters from AFTER DUTY until 2300

....
Adjutant for Commanding Officer.

Initials of Flight or Section Officer.

Valid during the year ....1939.... up
to last day of Each Month.

Month	Initials	Month	Initials
Jan.		July	
Feb.		Aug.	
Mch.		Sep.	
Apl.		Oct.	
May		Nov.	
June		Dec.	

(1881—5) Wt. 39566—3105 25,704 2/39 T.S. 700
(2815—5) Wt. 15496—877 92,736 6/39 T.S. 700

till it was time to try and get a lift back to camp. I thought I might get a lift with a milkman or something, and set off to walk through the snow only to suddenly realise that it was now Christmas Day and there would be no milk deliveries, so I carried on walking, never saw a soul, man or beast, and finished up walking all the way back to camp, doing the 1st half mile across the airfield so that I didn't have to go past the guardroom and be clobbered for being out late, very late.

On January 18th, 1940 it was my 21st Birthday, a day I will never forget. My sister had made and sent me a birthday cake. After lunch I collected it from the Station Post Room, took it back to the billet, opened it up, had a piece myself and gave a piece to my immediate mates in the room, it wasn't big enough to go round everybody. The remainder I put back in the tin and put it away in my kit box and went to work. After work and the evening meal, I returned to the billet, opened up my cake tin to enjoy a piece of fruit cake before going on guard mounting parade (I'd been detailed for guard duty that night) but to my dismay and disgust the cake had vanished. I never found out who had stolen it, I wish I had, but it was the first time I had seen any thieving during nearly three years service. I remember being very upset about it and even now I have very little enthusiasm for birthday celebrations. To spend ones 21st. wandering round the hangars with a pickaxe handle over my shoulder and feeling very downcast has put me off birthdays for ever.

A few weeks after that episode, both 35 and 207 squadrons were on the move yet again, this time to R.A.F. Upwood which again was an older station, near the small town of Ramsey, not far from either Peterborough or Huntingdon. There both squadrons were disbanded, on paper, and jointly re-formed as No 17 O.T.U. (Operational Training Unit). Our Fairey Battles were taken away and replaced by Bristol Blenheims and Avro Ansons as training aircraft. Upwood became quite interesting (for me at least), we had our first air raid.

One night during night flying practices, a German bomber dropped a number of small bombs along the flare path. Some of them were fitted with some sort of siren which made a hideous screaming noise as they fell. Luckily, no one was injured except a tractor driver, and him only slightly, and very little damage was done except to the tractor he was driving, and that too was slight. While the raid was on, most of us had been ordered down into the air raid shelters which were actually beneath the barrack block, although, as it happened, we need not have done so. The following day I picked up a small piece of shrapnel, obviously a piece of one of the bombs casing. I still have it somewhere.

While I was at Upwood I was sent on a gun turret course to a factory in Coventry, as Blenheims were fitted with a gun turret for the wireless operator/air gunner. Then one day I went on a flight in a Blenheim on a test flight after servicing, to check turret operation in flight, not gun firing. We flew westwards for some time, and then after a few gentle aerobatics we started back to base, but after a minute or so the pilot must have realised he was lost, he looked for and saw a railway line and not far away a country station, went down and banked over so he could read the name of the station, a quick check on his map, found out where he was and followed the line home. Fortunately, it was in the days before station names were hidden from aerial view to confuse the enemy, or so it was thought.

In early May 1940, 1 was awarded my first Good Conduct stripe for three years good conduct obviously, which meant an extra 3d. a day and as it was always jokingly put, for three years undetected crime. Then in June I took the stripe down and put two up instead as I was promoted Corporal and became a member of the Corporals Club, one step away from the holy of holies, the Sergeants Mess.

The Battle of Britain, as it became known, did not affect us very much as our aircraft were not involved and we were too far from London or other big cities to warrant attention from the Luftwaffe, and after that first raid they left us alone. Most of our off-duty days were spent in Peterborough or Huntingdon with the occasional 48 hour pass in London.

However, all good things come to an end, and in early November I was suddenly posted to R.A.F. Debden in Essex, Battle of Britain station, which made me wonder what next? On arrival there late one Friday evening, I found that I had joined a number of other men of various ranks and trades, and that we were posted to 73 Fighter Squadron (ex B of B) and that the Sqdn was going overseas. Actually, most of the Sqdn personnel were already on one week's embarkation leave, and those of us who had just arrived were told that if we wanted leave, we could go on Saturday morning, or that night if we wished, but had to be back on camp by mid-day Sunday.

There wasn't time to go home, and I did not feel like sitting around twiddling my thumbs for a day and a half, so I went to London to see a girl friend I knew to say cheerio. I left Debden about 9.00am but did not get to London until nearly 1.00pm due to hold-ups on the line because of air raids or bomb damage on or near the line. It took me till nearly 4.00pm to find her.

She and her parents had been bombed out of their home three times and rehoused each time, so I had no address to go to, but I finally found her at work, she was a typist at the Admiralty, and was just about to leave for the day.

I met her as she was leaving and we went to her latest home in Islington, had tea, and then with her mum and dad, all four of us went down the air raid shelter for the night. This shelter was in one of Whitbreads, the brewers deepest cellars in the building where her father worked during the day. This sort of thing seemed to be the normal habit for many people during the blitz, thousands used to go down into the Underground stations for safety. Next morning we all went back to her home, had breakfast and then went straight to Liverpool Street Railway Station, where we said goodbye, and got on the train back to camp. And that was my embarkation leave, all twenty seven hours of it.

Back at Debden however, things were moving more slowly, for all the 'panic stations' on Friday night. We were partly kitted out with some K.D. (khaki drill), given medical inspections, and more injections, indicating we were going somewhere warm, or even hot, waited around for long periods and finally left Debden by train for somewhere, by Tuesday mid-day. After countless halts, diversions and delays we arrived on Glasgow docks late Wednesday afternoon, and went aboard a large vessel moored at the quayside.

This was a freighter which had been taken off the North Atlantic meat run and converted into a troopship called FRANCONIA. For the coming trip, its load consisted of the ground crews of three squadrons, 37 and 38 Bomber and 73 Fighter. Even at this point, we still had not been told where we were going. The holds of the ship had been cleaned out and fitted out as mess decks, with rows of two tiered bunks like shallow boxes, and in between the bunks were long tables and forms secured to the decking. Above these tables, hooks were fixed to the ceiling beams and from these hooks, people not in bunks slung hammocks to sleep in. It was quite crowded really.

Sometime during the night, the Franconia slipped her moorings and headed off down the river Clyde. Next morning, going up on deck all we could see was a cloudy sky and heaving water in every direction. The sea was not really rough, but considering it was winter, it was not particularly calm either, and very soon, sea sickness began to affect many of us. Although we did not know it at the time, but we found out later, that we had left the Clyde, sailed north and then west out into the Atlantic, and then down past Ireland and headed for the bay of Biscay. It was also apparent that we were part of a convoy protected by a number of Naval vessels, one of which was the aircraft carrier H.M.S. Furious.

After two days at sea, I had found my sea legs and recovered from mild sea sickness, when I went sick with tonsillitis and was admitted to the sick bay, where I was under medication for about three days. During this time I had become friendly with the medical Cpl. who, it appeared was to be our squadron medic when we reached our destination. He suggested, when I had recovered, that if I wanted to stay in the sick bay, instead of going back to the mess deck, I could, the sick bay being nearly empty and it would be much more comfortable there, and I could move about a bit and be less likely to be grabbed for guard duties, boat drills etc.

One day while still in the bay of Biscay we were sailing parallel with and about 3-400 yards away from the starboard side of the Furious. Some of her aircraft, Fairey Fulmars, were doing take-offs and deck landings. Suddenly, as one Fulmar touched down on the flight deck, it's starboard undercarriage leg collapsed and the aircraft slewed to one side and shot straight over the edge of the flight deck and into the water with scarcely a splash and disappeared.

Convoys never stop in war time no matter what happens, and Furious steamed on, as a couple of destroyers came racing up from the rear of the convoy to search for survivors, if any. We heard later that one man had been picked up, but whether pilot or air gunner, we never found out, or whether the second crew member was ever found.

After about ten days of zig-zagging first one way and then the other to avoid the possibility of submarines presumably, we finally turned eastward and headed, as it turned out for Gibraltar. Part of the convoy including Franconia went into Gib. as it is usually known, harbour while the remainder carried on southwards, probably heading for Freetown or Cape Town. We were only in Gib. for about a day and a half so didn't get a chance to go ashore and climb the rock and see the sights and the apes, which is what most visitors seem to do on a Gib. holiday these days. Apparently we were joining and forming the first convoy to go through the Med. after Italy entered the war.

It seemed that the three squadrons on Franconia were urgently needed in Egypt in the Western Desert for use against the Italian Forces and this was the quickest way to get them there. Personnel were divided between two cruisers, H.M.S. Manchester and H.M.S. Southampton. The Admiral in charge of the convoy flew his flag on the Manchester, so she was the flagship of the convoy. All 73 Sqdn and half 38 Sqdn ground crew were to be accommodated on the Manchester while Southampton took the remainder of 38 and all 37 Sqdn.

We were housed mainly in the two hangars, one either side of the upper-structure which normally had a Walrus amphibian aircraft in each one. These were to be flown off to make room for us. One was, the other was unserviceable, so, no messing about, it was taken from the hangar, its underside stove in by a large pointed tool, lifted by a crane, slung out over the side and dropped into the water where it quickly sank. What a waste we thought, but in wartime, time is more important than long repairs to an aircraft. I've often wondered if it is still at the bottom of the harbour.

Those of us who could not find space in the hangar were spread around the ship in all sorts of odd corners. Two other Cpls and myself slept on a blanket on the steel floor of the electricians workshop at night. It was a hard mattress. By day, we wandered round the ship trying to keep out of the way of busy sailors. We left harbour under the cover of darkness, and when we surfaced in the cold light of day, all we could see was a number of ships of various sizes and lots and lots of water and hoped for an interesting trip. We were not disappointed.

HMS Manchester

Each day and every day at 11.00 hours, a crowd of airmen used to gather on the deck above the Well Deck, I think it was called, to witness one of the oldest traditions of the Navy, or so we were told, the daily issue of the rum ration. At the appointed time, almost to the second, the Duty Officer of the day, his accompanying Petty Officer, a rating writer, and two other ratings appeared on the Well Deck amidships, with a small wooden cask of full strength rum and a quantity of water.

The rum was diluted with water to bring it to the correct strength. Then, ratings, one representative from each mess lined up with containers of various types and sizes to collect the rum ration for his respective mess, each one calling out the number of his mess which was noted by the writer. He then received his allotted ration. When all had been served, and woe betide any rep. who was late (he missed it), the remaining liquid, if any, in the container was to our horror and dismay, thrown over the side, under the very eyes of about a hundred and fifty thirsty airmen. This was also, alas, a Naval tradition and by law, no rum once removed from bond can be returned.

After about three days in the Med. going through the Straits of Pantellaria, we had a minor dust-up with several units of the Italian Fleet. Rather frightening and yet exhilarating in a way as we were only passengers, and to keep us out of the way of the Navy blokes, to let them get on with the fighting, we were battened down in the bathrooms and heads area. An excellent idea from the matelots point of view, but I shudder to think what might have happened, had we been hit by a bomb or a shell and no one could find the bloke with the key.

At one point during the skirmish, a hydraulic lift from the magazine, carrying shells up to one of the gun turrets broke down and some of us were hauled out of our shelter to take the place of the lift. This meant going into the magazine, collecting a shell, one between two men, as it felt as though it weighted a hundredweight, and probably did, and carrying it in a sort of plaited straw bag with a handle at each side up three flights of steps to the run turret. Fortunately, after two such trips, the guns ceased firing. The Italian ships had retreated rapidly and we heard later that none of the ships in the convoy had been damaged, but an Italian destroyer had been sunk and battleship damaged, but this was never confirmed. This engagement became officially known as The Battle of Cape Spartivento.

An amusing incident occurred after the foregoing events during the continuing voyage, in the 'heads' of one of the cruisers. This is hearsay, but I can well imagine it happening, considering the R..A.F. sense of humour. The 'heads' or toilet area are at the sharp end of the ship, the bows, in some ships anyway. They were two decks down below the main deck. Looking from the bow, the wash basins were along one side of the area, and the toilets along the other. The latter consisted of a number of small cupboard or cabin-like structures arranged in a row, over a long shallow metal trough of water. Each cabin had a wooden seat across its width with a hole in it to sit on, and a half door at the front so that feet could be seen, indicating occupancy, but the rest of the occupant shielded when seated. One morning when many of the cabins were occupied, some wit ignited a number of paper 'boats', and put them in the trough of running water. Naturally, with the motion of the ship, as the bow rose and fell, the water in the trough followed this movement, and went gently from one end to the other, first one way, and then the other, carrying the bits of burning paper with it and the sight of heads going up and down one after the other as the cabin occupants momentarily rose from their seats and subsided again in union must have been hilarious to behold. Luckily no one suffered any real damage except to pride, but it was never discovered who started it, someone with a warped sense of humour no doubt.

At last, after about a week or so going through the Med. we finally entered Alexandria Harbour and tied up alongside a quay during the night. A pity really, it would have been a much better sight going in by day. Anyway, we woke up one morning about the end of November and went out on deck in blazing sunshine to indescribable smells and sounds of (to us) the mystical east. We had arrived in Egypt, the farthest I, and many others had ever been away from home.

Some months later we (the Sqdn personnel) all got certificates saying we had been on H.M.S. Manchester during the previously described action, signed by the Captain. I still have mine. It was probably her first battle honours as a flagship.

Chapter 5

Africa

During the morning we disembarked with all our kit and belongings and boarded a train which ran along the quay and eventually left Alexandria for Cairo. The journey was like entering a new world, which it was, to most of us. Some of the older members of the Sqdns had been abroad before to places like India, Iraq, Palestine, Aden, Singapore and even Egypt itself, and were quite blase about the journey, but to some of us younger 'sprogs', it was an eye opening experience. We had several stops en route, and at every stop the train was besieged by hordes of young boys, and some not so young, all in their long night-shirt like apparel (Galabyas) or something like that, and most of them barefooted, trying to sell us all sorts of food and drinks, and cigarettes, but we were a little wary of their standard of hygiene. We passed through sandy areas, but most of the land near the railway appeared to be very fertile and productive with canals and ditches providing irrigation, camels, donkeys or bullocks providing the motive power to transfer water from canals to ditches.

We eventually arrived at Cairo, and after leaving the train boarded lorries and buses to take us to our new temporary home, R.A.F. Heliopolis, near Cairo suburb of the same name, and to a row of huts reserved for 73 Squadron. Personnel of 37 and 38 Sqdns were taken to some temporary accommodation where they would be housed for one night and continue to another station the next day, but I'm not quite sure which one they were heading for. Heliopolis was a pre-war permanent overseas station with several squadrons of (to some of us) fairly ancient aircraft, twin engined bi-planes such as Valencias, Virginias, the odd Bombay or two, and some single engined Lysanders, Hawker Hinds and Harts and even some Gladiators. We were to be there nearly a month before all our complement of Hurricanes arrived. They had gone to a West African port in crates, been unboxed, assembled and flown across Africa in stages. As they arrived we were very busy indeed preparing them for movement up to the desert airfield we were destined for, and eventual operational activity.

Until the aircraft arrived we had been kept occupied by being issued with further items of K.D., more inoculations, if required, physical training and drill to bring us up to a good state of fitness. We attended lectures on desert warfare, dangers of fires, health matters etc, and then in the afternoons we were free to leave camp and go into Cairo itself and marvel at the sights of a large smelly city with streets crowded with trams, camels, donkeys, gharrys (a sort of horse drawn open carriage, as numerous as London taxis, and serving the same purpose) and of course, the native population. Cars seemed to be rather scarce, compared with other road users, buses plentiful but not cars.

It was a beautiful city in some respects, particularly down by the river Nile with its houseboats, and out in the suburbs of quiet streets of large houses set in their own grounds, and one place we found to our liking, not too far from the camp, a roller skating rink, where some of us spent a lot of our leisure time. We got to know a few young people who lived nearby and also spent a lot of time at the rink. I think they were the sons and daughters of fairly well-off people who lived in Heliopolis, a modern suburb from which the camp had taken its name. One family we got to know were originally from Austria and spoke very good English. One girl said she spoke eight languages, but her brother admitted he was very poor linguistically, he only spoke five. We also went to see some pyramids out beyond one of the suburbs, a little way out into the desert. We went to some of the cinemas, quite palatial places, and several other sights of interest. Much of the inner city, was like some of the suburbs, unbelievably squalid, dirty and overcrowded.

We spent Christmas there on the camp in the traditional RAF manner, with the Officers and Senior N.C.O.'s serving the other ranks with their Christmas dinner, followed by the usual sing-song and impromptu concert.

At last everything was ready, and early on New Years Day 1941 our lorries were loaded, and off we went in convoy through the suburbs and out of Cairo on to the desert road northwards, which ultimately led to Alexandria. This was a good tarmac road, single carriage way, but wide and smooth, from which we turned left before reaching Alex, at a junction near the small village of Amerya which was now the western desert road as far as one could go. We stopped for a break at a N.A.A.F.I. canteen and then went on for a considerable way towards Mersa Matruh, probably a holiday resort before the war, but deserted now, with the inhabitants having gone back to Alexandria or Cairo no doubt. We passed Mersa Matruh and after a further good few miles, turned left again off the main road on to a minor road, little better than a track, away from the sea. and that petered out into a definite track which climbed up to a plateau, on which was the Airfield known as Sidi Haneesh. It was merely a large flat area of hard sand, which had been cleared of rocks, large stones and clumps of camel thorn by previous occupants, to make a landing ground with tented accommodation and messes off to one side.

The Officer's, Sergeant's and Airmen's messes were well separated and were rather dilapidated wooden buildings which had been erected and used by the Italian forces who had once held this place.

On arrival, the first task was to unload and erect a tent for my section, who would be working in the maintenance flight. Some distance away from the tent were the latrines, previously dug by the sanitation section. These were a bit of an eye opener as had the 'heads' been on the Manchester. A trench, some eight or nine feet long, about two feet deep and one and a half feet wide had been dug and surrounded by a hessian screen, about six feet high. At each end of the trench was a St. Andrews cross shaped wooden stand and between the two crosses was a long pole to sit on. Privacy inside the screen was non-existent. I do not think I've ever seen anything so primitive. At the end of the day, sand was shovelled into the trench to keep the flies at bay, and every second day a second trench was dug and the first one completely filled in.

Some aircraft were already there ready for operational use. Soon there were three separate areas of tents in rows, one for each flight nearest to their aircraft. Each tent held six to eight men. We slept on bedboards or on the ground, according to preference, and the amount of livestock in the sand, fleas, scorpions etc were rife and vicious. We kept our kit and kitbags beside us, and strung a rope between the tent poles to hang clothes and things on.

The first night was enlivened somewhat about eleven thirty by the clamour of fire alarm bells and shouts of FIRE! FIRE! and on looking out of the tent opening, we could see the Officers mess building was on fire. As we were a good distance away from it, and it was obvious there was nothing we could do to help, it being tinder dry, blazing away quite merrily and no water around, we went back to sleep again. Next morning there was nothing but a pile of ashes, but a new marquee was there and erected by lunchtime, so they were better off than we were after all.

Then began our war in earnest. Each day the Hurricanes flew sorties against Italian aircraft with considerable success. One day, two of our pilots shot down 6 C.R. 42s. The weather was reasonably kind, dry and cold at night, but the days were altogether different. Blue working dress was worn first thing in the morning, including greatcoats to go to breakfast in, but by ten o'clock we had changed into K.D. and the afternoons were warm enough to strip to the waist. There were the odd bad days when it actually rained, but not many, and days when we had sandstorms.

The worst conditions were during what was called a KHAMSIN, a hot dry wind coming straight up from the Sahara, carrying very fine dust, almost like talcum powder, not sand. When they were coming they were very obvious. From the southwest, a large black cloud appeared and came slowly towards us. When it arrived, there did not seem to be any wind at all, it just became stiflingly hot and more like a fog than anything else, but the dust settled on everything everywhere. In the mess at dinner, we were having rice pudding as a sweet, as usual, and the surface of the rice was quickly coated with dust and removing a spoonful to eat left a white patch, but by the time that spoonful was eaten, plus dust, and the spoon went back to the plate, the white patch was covered again. The dust got everywhere. It was like being in a thick fog but hotter. However work had to be done, although no flying could take place in a Khamsin, when it was over, back to work as usual, but more so because of the dust.

Harmonising the guns in a Hurricane cockpit

Our normal work consisted of servicing aircraft from the flights on normal periodic inspections, determined by the number of flying hours, removing and cleaning the eight 303 in. Browning machine guns from each aircraft, gauging components for wear and replacing where necessary, installing the guns back in the mountings in the wings. Meanwhile, engine fitters, riggers, and other tradesmen were busy on all the other aircraft systems. After gun servicing and installation, the guns had to be harmonised with the guns in the cockpit. This was my job, which was then checked by the pilot of the particular aircraft, or was by most of them for their own satisfaction, after all, their lives might depend on the accuracy of their armament. With over twenty aircraft to keep flying and serviceable, we did not have a lot of spare time. Any time off was usually spent going down to the beach which was within fairly easy reach to swim in the Med although I did not or could not pick up the art of swimming and never have done since.

One thing I did achieve though, very soon after our arrival in the desert, was to learn to drive a motor vehicle. This was necessary so that I could drive a truck in the course of my job. I learned the hard way. A Cpl. from the M.T. (motor transport) section took me in a three-ton Ford truck to the far side of the airfield, away from all danger of entangling with the aircraft, and first gave me a short lecture on driving, then demonstrated what he had told me, all about the engine and gearbox, starting and stopping, use of clutch and gearlever and how to operate them correctly, use and operation of brakes, hand and foot and having gone over all that at least three times, he then said, 'right, it's all yours. Practice and when you think you can do it, bring it back to the M.T. Section'. So there I was with a vehicle, plenty of petrol, half the western desert to do it in and could I do it? I did. After about two and a half hours of starting, stopping, changing up and down through the gears, reversing, steering with one hand while changing gear, in fact all that I had been told and shown, and by that time, I reckoned I'd got the hang of it, and went back to the M.T. Section Office. After a few days practising at odd times I was tested by the M.T. Sgt. and passed as fit to drive. I still have the piece of paper authorising me to drive Service Transport of No. 73 Squadron.

The only thing I had not been shown or had explained to me was the art of towing another vehicle, especially one with starting difficulty or a flat battery. Again I learned the hard way. One day, at our place of work, the Flt. Sgt. in charge of the maintenance Flight, told me to give the driver of another vehicle a tow to start it as it had a flat battery. I told him that I could not as I did not know how to do it properly, never having done it before and I was a novice driver, but he told me in no uncertain terms to do as I was told and get on with it. Needless to say, through sheer ignorance of towing by rope, I broke the rope twice. The Flt.Sgt. roundly and probably squarely too, cursed me in his usual inimitable manner which is unprintable, and told me to get out of the truck, and he would show me how it should be done. This he did very competently and without rancour, and when I tried again, I managed it perfectly well. I have never had the slightest trouble since, in doing a tow start, but I believe that nowadays the correct method is not towing but by using 'jump leads' from a vehicle with a good battery attached to the flat battery.

As time passed, the Italian Forces were retreating rapidly and to stay in touch with them we had to move forward as well to another airfield. We packed all our equipment, loaded our trucks and left to go further west, past Sidi Barani to Solumn where we spent the night. This was the last town in Egypt before the border. It had been a seaside resort too, but occupied by Italians who had abandoned it in their retreat.

There were plenty of empty houses, some of them comparatively undamaged, and with furniture still in them, so instead of bothering with tents we just parked by a house and moved in. They had been nice little houses, but one thing surprised us and that was the house toilet, the first one I had seen. It was the normal sized 'little room' but instead of the usual pedestal type of toilet we were used to, it consisted of a square porcelain shallow tray with a 5-6 inch diameter hole in the middle, and slightly in front of the hole, off-set one to each side were two footprint shaped indentations in the porcelain base. It was obvious what it was for, but how odd. I have since noticed that sort of toilet is standard in many places in eastern countries.

Next morning, up, breakfast and away again, up through the notorious Slumn Pass with its steep climbs and hair-pin bends, quite hair raising for a novice driver, perhaps even more so for the passengers in the cab, but I made it without mishap, and we went on to another Italian airfield called Sidi Omar, near Fort Capuzzo and the same living conditions applied as before.

Driving along the road, we noticed another strange sight, one which was to be repeated several times later. The Italian Army was surrendering by the thousand around this time and they were shipped on to places like Northern Rhodesia and Kenya where they were interned for the duration of the war. During one of our moves, as we drove along the road, there was a long column of prisoners walking the other way. There must have been several thousand of them and at the head of the column was a single British soldier and another at the rear, presumably to prevent escapes, and the soldier had given his rifle to an Italian to carry as we were passing. Not that they wanted to escape, they were only too happy to be out of it and still be alive. A lot of their friends were not.

More aerial successes and unfortunately a few losses over the next few weeks and then on the move again, past Bardia and Tobruk to yet another ex-Italian airfield, this time Gazala. It had some buildings on it and a hangar, and had obviously been evacuated in haste and recently. We joined up with a bomber squadron, No 55 I think who were flying Blenheims.

At Gazala we found a lot of Italian equipment abandoned in their haste to get away as they retreated further and faster to the west. Much of this equipment was in a serviceable condition, especially some of the transport, which when refuelled was in perfect working order. The fuel for these vehicles was there too. Several of our chaps found some motor bikes that had been left behind, and had a lot of fun with them when off duty.

There were also a lot of bombs of various sizes lying all over the place. Many of these were fused all ready for use and these had to be destroyed. The squadron Armament Flt. Sgt. had done a course on demolition of foreign, German and Italian bombs, so with my section to help him we had a rare old time blowing up these bombs, some before, some after defuzing.

After a fairly short stay at Gazala, as German reinforcements were appearing in strength in North Africa and advancing eastward, our forces started to retreat, the RAF included. Our squadron was due to go back to Sidi Omar, or even Sidi Haneesh. As this was beginning to take place, a small detachment of armourers and other ground tradesmen, including my section, 8 or 9 in all were detailed to go to a landing ground close to the sea and near Bardia to act as a refuelling and re-arming party to save our aircraft having to go all the way back to base between sorties, thus saving time against the advancing Germans.

We arrived at the deserted airfield and started erecting tents to live and work in, in the early afternoon. Shortly after our arrival, a sandstorm blew up and we could hardly see a thing. Next we heard an aircraft circling overhead, from the sound of the engine, a Hurricane. The aircraft seemed to fly out to sea and come back getting lower and lower until he was over the beach and touched down a short distance beyond. A tricky landing in a sandstorm, but he obviously knew the area, and all he had to do was cross the beach as low as possible and then let straight down on to the ground, and once down, the problem was locating him or he us.

However, there he was, and I do not know who found who. Apparently he had been told to try and find us and tell us to get out of there but fast, and back into Tobruk where the squadron was now positioned, as the Germans had captured Gazala and were winging round south towards Bardia and beyond to Solumn. He took off again and we immediately repacked our gear, loaded our three lorries and headed back into Tobruk to join up with the squadron again. We were told later that the Germans had entered Bardia early the following morning. But for that pilot's skill in landing, giving us his message, and taking off again in a sandstorm, I might not be writing this now. The first chance we had we bought him all the beer he could drink, a small sign of our appreciation.

Tobruk Harbour

Tobruk airfield was situated on a plateau overlooking the harbour from the south, and our only way out was by sea. We were there several days either side of Easter, and it was not very pleasant. One day, by sheer chance one of the squadron drivers took a wrong track looking for a way, if possible to the sea. He carried on along the track he was on and came across some cave entrances, not visible from anywhere except this track. Ideal for explosives storage or anything else if necessary. He stopped and went into one and found hundreds, maybe thousands of crates of mineral water, and showing great presence of mind, loaded his truck and brought it all back to camp. It was a godsend, for some time we had been a bit tight on drinking water, as the Italians had salted some of the wells in the desert as they retreated, which made the water practically undrinkable, and the ration became, half a pint per man, per day, perhaps. Every day as long as we were there, a truck load was brought into camp. We drank it, we made tea with it, we washed and shaved in it, and as someone remarked, the cooks even washed up with it. I have often wondered who got it when we left, or whether it was never found again.

It was quite a hairy time in Tobruk really, but interesting nevertheless. Tobruk itself, already in ruins, the harbour and the airfield were bombed daily at 7.00am, 12 noon, and 5.00pm regularly for over a week, always at meal times, it seemed, and occasionally at night. When it was not being bombed, shells from big guns, twelve miles away at Bardia, whistled overhead at intervals.

We seemed to spend more time with our heads down in our slit trenches than with them up. Luckily none ever fell short as they went right over the camp into the harbour.

One night, sometime after midnight, a Jerry bombed the airfield and dropped a stick of bombs across the area where we were sleeping and where our ammunition was stacked. The stick was fairly widely spaced and nothing happened to us as we had dashed into our slit trenches at the onset of the raid.

Next morning, when we got up to go to breakfast, there on the ground about thirty yards from our tent was an unexploded bomb. It was the middle one of the stick of five. Later we found two more similar bombs a couple of hundred yards away either side of our position. The only ones that had exploded were the first and last of the stick. When we checked the one near our tent, we found it wasn't armed properly. Neither were the other two, somewhere, somebody was looking after us that night.

A more pleasant memory of Tobruk was the holding of an Easter Sunday Holy Communion Service by the squadron C. of E. Padre. About thirty or so people attended. The Altar was an empty ammunition box covered by a white cloth with a Crucifix on it, and I remember the Padre had a white surplice over his K.D. shorts and desert boots. Oddly enough there were no air raids that day. Perhaps the Germans were having an Easter Service too. Even the big guns at Bardia were quiet as well.

Another amusing little memory I have of our time in Tobruk is of a small wire haired white terrier which had come from goodness knows where and attached itself to our Flt. Sgt. Discip. at one of the camps we were on and stayed with him. That little dog used to sense when an air raid was imminent. As soon as it became aware of a coming air raid, and it knew before the air raid siren sounded, it used to dig itself down into the sand, in other words, it dug its own little slit trench. Perhaps it could hear or sense the vibrations of aero engines running up at Gazala about 20 miles away.

But alas, or thank goodness, all good things, or bad, depending on ones point of view, come to an end sometime (I think I've said that before) and we had reached the end of the line, so to speak. We had lost all our aircraft, some in combat, others shot up on the ground, and as the powers that be obviously thought it would be futile to send any more, it was decided that we would have to be evacuated, and there was only one way out, by sea, but before I get to the evacuation I must mention our C.O., or rather our new C.O. and his arrival on the squadron. I hope I remember correctly, but it is along time ago.

He was Squadron Leader Peter Whickham-Barnes, an ex Halton apprentice I believe, who was, as quite a few A.A.s were, selected for aircrew training and went to Cranwell, the Royal Air Force College, was commissioned and was probably a Battle of Britain pilot. He came to join 73 as Commanding Officer and naturally came in his own aircraft and arrived right in the middle of an air attack. I hope I am right, but I am not 100% sure, and I trust he will forgive me if I am wrong, but he had his aircraft shot from under him in a manner of speaking, and landed at Tobruk by parachute. His stay there must have been comparatively short and presumably he was evacuated with the rest of us.

Then one afternoon, with only what kit we could carry in our haversacks, the rest we left or buried, we departed from Tobruk airfield. We left in lorries and were driven down through the ruins of the town to the harbour where in the middle of a lot of ships was one called Barpeta which was our target. She was an ammunition ship and was still being unloaded into barges when we arrived. We hung around on the dockside for a while and then a lighter came alongside the quay for us. We boarded it and were taken out and transferred to the Barpeta as quickly as we could as it was getting near 4 o'clock by this time. We sorted ourselves out and hoped the unloading would be finished before 5.00pm, the usual air raid time.

But no such luck. Dead on 5 o'clock the air raid sirens sounded, over came the Stukas (JU 87s) and down came the Stukas and the bombs. I had found myself a nice cosy spot under a metal deck housing covering some steps to a lower deck. On top of the housing was a sandbagged gun position with a Lewis gun mounted on it. All the short time that raid was on, that Lewis gun never seemed to stop firing. I stayed where I was in my little corner, and I don't mind admitting that I prayed. Anyway, prayers or not the raid ended and the attackers left. Whether any were shot down or whether any damage was done to any ships, I know not, but I was glad when it was all over. On land, if being bombed, one can try to evade being involved, but on a ship there is nowhere to go.

That evening about seven o'clock, we sailed for Alexandria and when clear of the harbour, we could see about being fed and explore the ship. To my surprise, and no doubt many others, we found that the holds had no covers over them, and they were full of Italian prisoners of war being taken to Egypt for onward travel to perhaps Kenya or Rhodesia, goodness knows when they were put aboard. As dusk began to fall, and we were well clear of Tobruk, the prisoners began to sing. They were so glad to be out of the war and still alive, they sang their hearts out, mostly in Italian, but some in English. They sang all the popular operas, and some not so well known, and some I had never heard of. We joined in when we could, which wasn't often. They sang in unison, in groups, solos, duets, full choir work, everything. I have never heard anything like it, before or since. They sang all night.

German and Italian high ranking prisoners being shipped off

We docked in Alexandria next morning, about eight months after our first landing, and what a memorable period it had been for me and perhaps all of us. We disembarked and this time boarded lorries to take us to our new base landing ground near Amerya where the rest of the squadron and our new aircraft awaited us. We sorted out our equipment and kit, replacing where necessary, and then headed back to where it had all started before, Sidi Haneesh.

Then followed a period of relative calm, sorties were carried out but many were mainly reconnaissance. Our work in maintenance was normal and the weather was much warmer now, especially in the mornings, but the food had not changed much, it was still bully beef and biscuits, one tin of beef and one packet of biscuits between two men, practically every meal. Occasionally we had tinned bacon for breakfast, but it wasn't very appetising, nor was the porridge we got for breakfast, also very occasionally. Our new C.O. was still with us and still well thought of by everyone. One day I had been doing a D.I. (daily inspection) on his Lysander communications aircraft, when he drove up in his big Humber staff car, got out and prepared to take off. He asked me to take his car back to his office tent, waved for me to remove the chocks in front of the wheels and off he went. I went across to his car, never having been near anything like that before, got in, started up and set off, but I could not resist a little spin round part of the airfield before going back to his office, He had gone, I thought, no one would be any the wiser, and I had enjoyed my little run.

A couple of weeks or so later I was passing him one day, and naturally saluted, he returned the salute, paused, and said with a twinkle in his eye, "what did I think about a Humber, compared with a three tonner?" I knew then that he had not been as far away as I had thought. I still remember him as one of the best C.O.'s I've had. He was definitely, as the saying goes, an Officer and a Gentleman and approachable. I never saw him again after I left the squadron, but he obviously survived the war, and some years afterwards, I used to see his name in the RAF News, now and then. He ended his career, I believe as AIR CHIEF MARSHAL Sir Peter Whickham, having dropped the Barnes part.

Not long after this episode, the Maintenance Flight moved to Amerya, and aircraft came down to us for their periodic servicing as required. We were in tents again but being a little nearer to civilisation, we had a few more creature comforts than we had out in the desert. Only four men in my tent now so we had a bit more room, the odd box or two to keep our stuff in, semi-permanent toilet facilities, a better water supply, slightly better, and certainly more varied food, fewer sandstorms and better time off allowances. And talking of food has reminded me of a rather amusing incident.

Referring to the last paragraph and item, varied food. We used to have a scheme where we all contributed a few piastres a week into a fund administered by the sqdn. Postal Cpl. and one of the Service policemen we had on the sqdn. Every other day or so, they used to go into Alex, in a truck to buy foodstuffs to implement our rations, extra messing, I think we used to call it, things like vegetables, fresh fruit, fresh bread etc, and one day they drove in as usual and parked in a side street just off Ramleh Square. They had done this often enough before, parked the truck, removed the distributor arm from the engine to prevent it being stolen (the Arabs were notorious thieves) and went off to do their shopping. Imagine their surprise and dismay, on their return to find the truck was still there, but it had been jacked up, bricks put under the axles and all the wheels removed. Hilarious to us when told about it, but not very funny to them. It took them a long time to live it down.

Another good point about near Alex, was that we could go there in our off duty time in a lorry or liberty bus as it was called. One night, having been to town for a night out at the pictures or playing 'housey' at the Fleet club, we were on our way back to camp when the air raid sirens sounded. Alex, suffered several air raids around this time mostly directed at the harbour and shipping, but sometimes a bomb went astray. That night we had just cleared the docks area when a stray mine fell on a built up area not far from the docks. From the back of the lorry we saw a huge flash and heard a loud explosion, and even though we were travelling away from it, we felt the heat from it and the blast, diminished by distance swept over us like a warm wind.

One of my main memories of my stay at Amerya, was the occasion when I fell ill with 'sand fly fever' they called it, and lying in the ambulance one morning awaiting transportation to Amerya sick quarters, when I heard people shouting, FIRE, and when I looked out of the ambulance windows, there, some distance away, blazing away quite fiercely was the armoury workshop tent. Apparently someone had been pouring petrol, which we used for gun cleaning (illegally, but more efficient than gun cleaning oil) when the petrol splashed on to a primus stove near the tent door opening, which was being used to boil water for tea and the whole lot went up in flames. Lucky for me that I was in the ambulance at the time, and was not involved at all at the subsequent court of inquiry.

Soon after this event, once I was fit again, the orderly room sent for me and told me I had been posted to 230 Squadron which was equipped with Sunderland flying boats (what a change from Hurricanes) and based at Abu Qir, on the coast east of Alexandria. The offices and workshops were situated just back from the beach, in peace time circumstances, just the spot for a seaside holiday, with aircraft moored in the bay. I was not on 230 very long but long enough to scrounge a trip in one of the aircraft on a test flight after servicing, a short one of only about 30 minutes but I quite enjoyed it.

I was also concerned, in a small way, in a rather odd incident. The Sunderland normally carried anti-submarine bombs or depth charges on its anti-submarine patrols. These were hoisted on to bomb carriers under the wings, and the carriers then retracted into the fuselage until required for use. On this occasion it was a test hoist and the charges were not armed. During the hoisting procedure, one of the depth charges had been hoisted and had just been attached to the carrier, when for no accountable reason, it fell off, straight through the bottom of the bombing scow. (I should have said that any work of this nature being done outside a Sunderland on the water, is usually done from a boat or scow). It was the last of the four being loaded, and naturally the scow sank.

The water was not terribly deep, but deep enough, and someone on board the aircraft threw me a rope and hauled me on board. All the other people involved could swim so did not need assistance. Actually, the 'unofficial' way to 'bomb up' was much simpler and easier, but just as effective. A crew of three men were used in the scow. The Cpl. in charge was called MacSpadyen, a burly Scot with the shoulders of an ox, a large ox. he would bend down in the scow, the other two would lift the charge and lay it across his shoulders, he then straightened up with the charge still on his shoulders and it was just the right height to secure the carrier hook to the lug of the depth charge. One of the team checked the hook test pin for security, and Mac stepped out from beneath it. Much faster and easier than with winches, but probably not legal in official eyes.

Sunderlands were also used for evacuating troops from Crete during that debacle, and one story of this said that on one occasion the aircraft had eighty five people on board, and it took a five mile take-off run before it could lift off. A Sunderland was used to bring a senior Yugoslav Officer, the C in C Yugoslav forces, General Mihailovic, I think, and his staff to Egypt.

It was not very long after this when , being the last arrival, I was posted or detached to another unit further along the beach. This unit had just arrived from Palestine, and was No 2 Yugoslav Squadron which was equipped with six Dornier 22 Seaplanes of German manufacture. Apparently, when the Germans invaded Yugoslavia, a number of Service personnel, rather than surrender, escaped with their aircraft and equipment, and made their way to Amman in Palestine. There, army personnel were formed into a unit and sent up into the Western Desert. The remainder, a mixture of Airforce and Fleet Air Arm personnel formed a squadron at Amman and were sent to Egypt, to Abu Qir together with their aircraft to carry out anti-submarine patrols in the vicinity of the approaches to Alex, harbour.

In addition to their aircraft, they also brought with them overland, two beautifully equipped workshop lorries containing the finest set of workshop tools and equipment, all in shadow drawers, I have ever seen, and some highly skilled and capable fitters who could do almost any job on an aircraft. They also brought a bus with them as a means of transport. With the Yugoslavs, there was an Englishman and his wife, both teachers in Yugoslavia before the war, who had escaped with them. On arrival in Palestine both had volunteered for service with British Forces, they would have been called up anyway, being English. Both were commissioned, Mr Sykes as liaison officer with the Yugoslavs being Yugoslav speaking while Mrs Sykes became officer in charge of W. A.A.F. personnel at Abu Qir Station.

There were also five or six RAF personnel of various ranks and trades posted in to the squadron to act as go-betweens in any dealings with RAF stores, workshops etc. The corporal clerk in the orderly room was actually born of Maltese parents in Egypt and spoke umpteen languages, or so it seemed, and naturally Arabic was one of them, and he was very useful in dealing with any outside matters with local tradesmen and people. I was the Armament N.C.O. of course and I soon found out the reason for my being there. The Dornier bomb carriers had two weapon suspension points, our anti-submarine bombs had only one bomb lug, so a small modification was necessary to the airframe to enable our bomb carriers to be attached to the airframe. I got together with the Yugoslav Warrant Officer engineer and an interpreter, explained what was required, and hey presto, in two or three days he had solved the problem, designed and made new mountings. These were fitted, our carriers mated to them, and with only the slightest bit of filing here and there, the job was done. Electrical services were incorporated, as the old method of release had been mechanical, and with the necessary fusing and release switches presenting no problem, loading and release tests were carried out successfully on an aircraft out of the water on the beach for routine servicing. With an aircraft suitably modified, work was put in hand to modify the other five aircraft.

While this work was being done, I had to train a team of young Yugoslav mechanics as makeshift armourers to be able to test and fit fuses to anti-submarine bombs, loading and unloading bombs to and from aircraft, defuzing bombs etc.

Working on the Dorniers in the water

This turned out to be very simple and easy in view of the language difficulty I thought I might have. One of the team selected for me turned out to be the ideal choice. He was a mere lad of no more than seventeen or so, and had been born in Alex, and spoke perfect English as well as his native tongue, and probably several other languages too. His family were in some sort of commercial business and lived in Cairo, where, because of the war, they had decided to settle permanently. The young boy had joined the Yugoslav Forces for patriotic reasons presumably. I made him my No. 2 and anything I said was immediately translated to the rest of the team, and vice versa for any queries. We carried out a dummy run on land several times to make them familiar with the operation, and then another one with the aircraft on the water, repeated several times. Then with the C.O. the team and myself satisfied that they could cope all right, the next move as to load an aircraft with unarmed weapons and have a test flight which was declared successful, and finally came the crunch, a live drop in the sea.

This time I flew with the pilot and bomb aimer, ostensibly to ensure the correct release procedure was carried out, besides I fancied a trip in a seaplane. It turned out to be quite exciting. I sat in the Air Gunner's position in the rear seat, but being an open cockpit, I could see through to where the Bomb Aimer was seated. We carried three 250lb antisubmarine bombs and an aluminium sea marker as the target. This was a packet of aluminium powder which, when dropped on the water, burst on impact and formed a round silvery circle on the surface, easily visible from above (this was standard practice for RAF bombing exercises at sea). We then climbed to about 6,000 feet and then went screaming earthwards in a very steep dive, just the way the German Stukas used to do. I squatted in my seat watching to see the right switches were operated in the correct order.

Suddenly the bomb was released and fell away and the pilot pulled out of the dive and reversed the direction of flight. I wasn't really expecting this, and I must admit it felt rather weird, but obviously dive bombing was their normal way of dropping bombs. Their instructors must have been German originally. The next two bombs were dropped in a similar fashion, but by now it did not seem quite so 'hairy' and I had learned to trust my monkey chain which secured me to my seat. None of the bombs actually hit the target but they were not very far away and the last one was very close indeed. Had it been for real, I think we might have claimed a 'kill'. But it wasn't and we didn't. We then returned and landed at Abu Qir bay and the landing too was somewhat surprising.

I suppose I was expecting a soft smooth landing, but no, water of course is incompressible and we hit it with a resounding clang. It sounded just like landing on concrete with the metal floats, not rubber tyres. I quite enjoyed the trip, but never had the opportunity for another one unfortunately. After a few more training flights for all the crews to familiarise themselves with the new system, the squadron was declared operational and commenced regular dawn and dusk patrols over the approaches to Alex, harbour. These continued for some months but no sightings of subs, were reported, and then one day on the dawn patrol we had our first casualties. While on patrol the aircraft flew over a Norwegian freighter, and for some unknown reason, when challenged by a Very pistol flare, fired an answering flare of the wrong colour. Naturally, with the aircraft being of German manufacture, the ships gun crews opened fire immediately and the aircraft was shot down. Only one of the crew survived. One of the two killed was a particular friend of mine which was a distinct shock. I had become quite good friends with a number of members of the Sqdn and spent a lot of time trying to teach them some English, and in return learned quite a bit of Serbo-Croat, most of which I have forgotten now.

I must say that I enjoyed my time with the Squadron. I had a tent to myself down on the beach not far from the water and made it nice and comfortable inside. I had to be fairly handy most of the time, just in case anything went amiss with the weapons, and I could not leave my team for too long, after all they were still just learners really. We were within easy reach of Alex, and public transport was readily accessible, so I was able to go there when I was off duty, to the cinema or the Fleet Club (a Naval establishment in pre-war days, now a bit like a glorified N.A.A.F.I. where one could get a good meal cheaply, and play 'housey' or bingo as it is called now. There was also accommodation for people on leave). But I digress, back to the Yugoslavs. Incidently, it will have been noticed that I have spelt Yugoslav the way it is pronounced, with a 'Y'. In fact, it was spelt with a 'J' in those days, but as J in Serbo-Croat is pronounced as a Y, the spelling seemed to change as well after the war. I hope that clears it up.

The Yugoslavs were quite a mixed bunch really, they came from all the different States which formed Jugoslavia after World War 1. Some were royalists, some were Communists, some were nothing at all politically, but they all remained on reasonably friendly terms with each other, or so it seemed until one day something happened politically which upset quite a number of them. I never did find out what the real reason for discord was, but it must have been pretty serious, as it resulted in operations being temporarily suspended, and the aircraft were brought out of the water and up on to the beach.

This state of affairs looked like continuing for some time and the jobs of the RAF detachment seemed to come to an end, and in my case, instead of going back to 230 Squadron, I was offered the chance to volunteer as an instructor in the Rhodesian Air Training Group, which as I had never been there, sounded interesting, I took, and regretfully said farewell to my Yugoslav friends and RAF colleagues who were also dispersed to other units in the Command.

We came now to the day when I departed from Abu Qir, together with two other chaps who were also bound for Rhodesia as trainee pilots. We went by train from Alexandria to Cairo, spent a night in a small transit camp, then next morning on another train to Port Suez at the southern end of the Suez Canal. There we joined other people also bound for Southern Africa and were taken by bus to the embarkation point where we boarded a sort of passenger boat (probably used in peace time for pleasure cruises) which took us out into the harbour to a monstrous black passenger ship which turned out to be the ILLE de FRANCE, a French luxury liner in peace time, which had been converted into a troopship capable of carrying several thousand troops. Our accommodation was spartan, to say the least, as are all troopships, each of the many decks equipped with tables and forms screwed to the deck with hammocks suspended from hooks in the ceiling for sleeping.

As well as our little group, there were a lot of troops going home to the UK, some having completed their overseas tours of up to five years, or more in some cases. Some were people who had been wounded in the desert, partly recovered and fit to travel home for further treatment. Some were in wards on the upper decks as hospital cases, and quite a lot were bound for aircrew training in Rhodesia or South Africa. In addition, there were a number of wives whose husbands were already in England, or had been posted to other Commands, and a few actually accompanying their husbands home. Some of the wives had children with them. There must have been upwards of 5,000 passengers on board, plus the crew.

That evening the anchor was raised and we sailed southwards. We soon got into the ships routine of eating, sleeping, playing cards, sunbathing, boat drills etc, but a number of us, mainly RAF were hijacked into volunteering for duty as gun crews on 6 pounder anti-aircraft guns. This was because we were going through the Red Sea and into the Indian Ocean, where Japanese ships or U-boats could be lurking. We had no Naval escort, relying on our speed to get us out of trouble, should anything occur.

As we went southwards, the weather became warmer and then the further we went, unbearably hot, almost too hot to play cards. We passed Aden, out of the Gulf of Aden and into the Indian Ocean and crossed the Equator almost un-noticed, none of the usual fun and games associated with this event. Once south of the line, the temperature dropped slightly, but the boredom remained. Being in 'almost enemy waters' the ship was blacked out at night. Those of us in gun turrets worked in shifts, 4 hours on and 8 hours off each day and night. We sailed on past Madagascar, and finally on to Durban, arriving there early in the morning.

We were allowed off the ship that day but had to be back on board by 22.00 hours. During that first day we walked into Durban from the docks as we needed the exercise after nearly two weeks at sea. We stopped on the way, when we came to a fish and chips cafe and had a meal. They tasted wonderful, the first fish and chips for nearly two years. Our first impressions of Durban were that it was a lovely town or city, I'm not quite sure which it is, with wide streets, clean and some splendid architecture in keeping with its position, and an opulent looking Shopping Centre..

One good thing we discovered was the Jewish Club. This was a kind of up-market canteen run and subsidised by the local Jewish Community, making it a social club for servicemen in uniform, living or stationed in the area, or like us, passing through. They held dances, had a good reading room, and a large room which was the restaurant where one could get an excellent meal for a shilling (5p). In 1989, when I was back in South Africa for the second reunion of the Wartime Air Training Scheme personnel, I visited Durban for three days, and though the city itself was hardly recognisable, with all the building and development that had gone on over the years, I found the Jewish Club again, still in the same place and still going, but its role seemed to have changed a bit, although it was still a club. Physically, it had hardly changed at all and I was made very welcome. They showed me a lot of photographs of its activities during the war, but I wasn't on any of them.

Back to 1942, later the first evening, just before dark, my mate and I were talking to two South African people we had met, and they invited us to have dinner with them at the Cumberland Hotel where they were staying on holiday from Johannesburg. We enjoyed a most sumptuous meal with them, after the monotony of ships fodder, I still have the menu. They invited us to go and see them again if ever we were in Johannesburg. We then went back to the ship again with the city in total darkness, as it was the first night of Durban's black-out, imposed after rumours that Japanese submarines were off the coast and could shell the city.

The next day, those of us who were staying in Southern Africa were disembarked and taken by bus to Clairwood transit camp. This was a tented camp with a large wooden dining hall, and a N.A.A.F.I., the tents being in lines separated by washing places (out-door) and toilets. We were split into groups, those going to South African flying training stations in one area, and a much smaller area for those going to Kenya or Southern Rhodesia. We had to parade every morning for roll call and those who were due to leave were singled out. The remainder were free for the rest of the day.

It became rather boring for some of us, as we were having a long wait for our actual postings, in fact, in our tent there were four of us going to Rhodesia who had to wait five weeks for our train reservations to Buluwayo. Time dragged a little but we filled it in by walking to Durban, going to the pictures, dances, or the Jewish Club and walking back at night. Very occasionally there was a concert or show on at the City Theatre. Through the Jewish Club some of us became friendly with South African families and were invited to their homes for a meal and a chat, especially those who had not been out there very long from England, and liked to talk about it. One family I met came from Tyneside, and with me just down the road, in a manner of speaking, we had plenty to talk about. At last we got our postings and our rail tickets, said our goodbyes to the Jewish Club and anyone else we knew, and were taken to the station. My ticket was right through to Salisbury.

South African trains are rather different from English ones. The engines seemed to be bigger and some had a water tender front and rear. Each carriage had a letter, a number or a name by way of identification and had a corridor running its full length, with an open observation platform at each end.

It was divided into compartments, the two end ones holding up to three people, and the remainder six. The reason for this arrangement was because they were sleepers as well as day carriages, as many of the journeys could not be completed in a day. Each side of the compartment became three bunks at night. The seat formed one,, the back of the seat hinged upwards and became another, while a third one hinged down from the back. Thus on the longer overnight journeys, these bunks were numbered sleeping positions, and when seats were booked, the ticket had a carriage identification, a compartment number and a seat number in the compartment. Consequently, on long journeys, compartments were all male or all female, at least at night. The three bunk compartments at each end were usually used by married couples or females only. Each evening around nine o'clock, native stewards came around making seats into beds by bringing sheets and pillows in and next morning came round again and cleared everything away. Each trip must have had a pretty hefty laundry bill.

The journey from Durban to Johannesburg (Jo'burg from now on) took all day, so we did not need beds, but on changing trains at Jo'burg, latish in the evening, beds were already being prepared when we boarded the train. I do not remember much about the trip from Durban, other than the first part was through cultivated and obviously fertile land, and then up through the mountains to the plateau of the hinterland. Then we left Jo'burg in the semi-darkness, so we did not see much of the countryside until daylight, and then it was nothing much to write home about. The area through which we were travelling was flat, monotonous land, almost desert-like, which the local people called 'bundu'. We spent most of the day playing cards or just staring out at nothing. It was a single track railway line with a loop line to allow for passing trains, every few miles. Water and fuel stops were fairly frequent. The train pulled up alongside a hanging pipe which was inserted into the water tender and water was taken on board. Some of the water stops had piles of logs beside the track so a supply of fuel could be taken on board as well. Once or twice I noticed that we pulled up and put water into tanks beside the line. This must have been a particularly arid area where water was scarce even for drinking.

After the best part of two days, we reached Buluwayo in the Southern Rhodesia, and here we changed trains for the last leg of the trip to Salisbury, the capital, a mere three hundred miles or so through countryside, much of it similar to that we had just left. Here we left the train and boarded a truck which took us to R.A.F. Belvedere, some five or six miles away. This was an Elementary Flying Training School (E.F.T.S.), and was also the transit camp for people like myself going on to other stations in the Group. It was also the Headquarters of the Rhodesian Air Training Group at that time but I believe they moved to Crambourne later. I was there for a week, pottering about and getting acclimatised, visiting Salisbury, a beautiful, modern, open city with wide streets lined with, mainly bungalows set in their own gardens. There was a very pleasant shopping area and several hotels, bars etc. in the city centre. The main streets in all Rhodesian towns were very wide indeed, built that way, it was said, in the days of the bullock carts, .when the streets had to be wide enough to turn a sixteen span of oxen round in them. Apparently you cannot reverse oxen.

The Rhodesians were like the South Africans, very hospitably inclined towards the British airmen, and this was obvious by the way cars used to queue at the guardroom gate on Friday afternoons to take people, any rank, out to their homes in the city or out to farms in the country and entertain them for the weekend. They might be taken game shooting, fishing in one of the few small lakes in the vicinity, or taken sight-seeing to places like the Matopos, or the Zimbabwe Ruins, or as a lot did, just sat around having a beer and talking about the places in England where they or their families came from originally. Some fellows who had been out there quite a while met and married girls they first met on weekend visits. After the weekend, they were brought back to camp on Saturday night or even Sunday morning. Being only a short stay there, I missed out on the proffered hospitality, but I found out later that it applied to other stations too.

At last I got my actual Station posting, this time to RAF Moffat near the town of Gwelo. So off I went again, back down the line I had so recently come up on to Salisbury. Not a long journey, only about 170 miles to Gwelo, known as the capital of the Midlands, in the middle of a large farming area. From the railway station to the camp was by the usual truck to take me the mile or so there. It was a hutted camp built purely for the purpose it was there for, temporary housing for the personnel of a training station, with the barrack square in the middle of the domestic area. At one side, some distance away was the Officers Mess and Quarters, while on the opposite side was the Sgts Mess and Quarters. The area on one of the other sides was taken up by the Airmen's Dining Hall, the N.A.A.F.I. with the Corporals Club, and the airmen's living accommodation. At the fourth side there was a large hut which was used as a church, more wooden buildings which housed Station Headquarters, Station Sick Quarters, and a whole block of huts which formed the Training School area, Orderly Room, Classrooms, and bombing teachers, and beyond these the Technical Site, with its workshops, main stores, parachute section, Armoury, 25 yard range etc, and after these the hangars and airfield and then only 'bundu'.
The training school gave the station its title, No. 24 Combined Air Observers School (C.A.O.S.). This was there I was to be employed.

Not long after I arrived, someone high up the command ladder must have taken a dislike to the name of the school, probably because of the letters (can't say that I blame him) and the school was renamed, 24 Navigation, Bombing and Gunnery School (N.B.&.G.S.). Sounded much better.

SGT's Mess RAF Moffat 1944

Gwelo was quite small really, with a white population of just over a thousand, or thereabouts, with a similar number of coloured inhabitants, mostly native African, but some of Indian origin. The town consisted principly of a main street, which led from the railway station, with several smaller streets off to each side, to junction where the left turning, after a few houses went out into the country of farms and more farms and on eventually to Buluwayo, a hundred plus miles away. Straight on led into the native area where we were not supposed to go. A right turn from the junction also led out into the bundu for about four miles to R.A.F. Thornhill, and then a further 30 miles or so to R.A.F. Guinea Fowl near the small town of Selukwe. Both of these were flying training stations.

The other way out of town from the railway station also went out into the country past the turn off to Moffat and eventually through QueQue and Gatooma, two gold mining towns, to Salisbury. The town had one large department store (Meikles) which sold almost everything, several smaller shops such as chemist, haberdashery, hairdressers, jewellers, bakers, shoes etc. There were two hotels, one with a cinema attached and a small hospital. Not a very exciting place on the face of it. There was a church and a chapel, but I'm sorry to say I never went to either of them.

Because Gwelo was a small town, with a small population, young ladies were a scarce commodity, and with two camps nearby, weekly dances held in the church hall seemed to consist of a dozen or so girls, and a hundred or more men, and every dance seemed to be, or became, an 'excuse me'. The hotel bars closed at 8.00pm and the cinema opened at that time. I think the idea of early bar closing, could mean people would drink less in the available time the bars were open. In fact they probably drank more by drinking faster. We were forbidden to mix or fraternise, as it was called, with the native population at all. If anyone was caught fraternising, they were off the camp, and out of the country, and sent home to England, or to India, usually the latter, at three or four hours notice. A posting to India was usually a sufficient deterrent.

As in the Salisbury area, the Rhodesians in and around Gwelo were very hospitably inclined, and we had lots of invitations to visit people in their homes. We also had quite a lot of hospitality from some of the farmers in the vicinity, who, because of their isolation, did not have many visitors from one month end to the next. Some of them lived well out into the country, and one place I used to visit was a small gold mine out in the Bundu towards Salisbury. On one occasion when I was there with another chap, we were taken out for a drive to a nearby farm to see if there was any game about. We didn't see much at all, and then we found out why. Going round a bend in the road, we approached some large rocks or boulders, set back a bit from the road, and sitting sunning themselves among these rocks was a whole pride of lions. There must have been six or seven of them of various sizes. They seemed friendly enough at a distance, but we drove past without slowing or stopping. It seemed prudent to do so.

Looking back on those days and comparing them with life in war-time England, life there was like being on a holiday camp. There was no black-out, very little rationing except petrol. Some English goods were scarce, in particular, whisky, but South African and Rhodesian beer was plentiful and Cape brandy replaced whisky for those who liked to drink the hard stuff. Fresh fruit was abundant, in fact there wasn't much we were short of except home comforts and plenty of girls to dance with, especially for us young single blokes.

There were other pastimes though. I started playing hockey again and actually got into the station team. Our away games were at either Thornhill or Guinea fowl nearby, or at stations near Buluwayo, in the south or Salisbury in the north. The latter were usually at weekends, which meant going there on Friday night, staying on one of the camps, games on Saturday and Sunday with a bit of drinking in between, and back on Sunday night.

That was the country, now what about the job I had gone there to do. Never having done any instructing before, I was assigned to 'sit-in' with one of the established instructors who was introducing would-be Air Gunners into the mysteries of the Lewis, Browning and Vickers 'K' guns, all of which they would be concerned with later. I knew all about these weapons of course, but the art of teaching other people about them was new to me, so I had to see and learn how it was done. I 'sat-in' with various instructors during the next few weeks, gradually taking a lesson or two to get the hang of it and eventually was given a class of my own for a full course.

In addition to weapons, they had to learn signalling, morse code, radio and Aldis lamp, aircraft recognition, from all angles, practice gun firing on the 25 yard range, clay pigeon shooting to help co-ordinate hand and eye, and of course, at last, air firing. First at ground targets from an aircraft flying low over them, and then air to air firing at a drogue or sleeve being towed by another aircraft, all of which they were tested on to assess their capability. If they proved satisfactory in all subjects, they were awarded the half- wing A.G.s flying badge and promoted to the rank of Sergeant, before being posted to an operational training unit, normally in England, although I believe some went to Kenya to an O.T.U there.

It was about this time that I became 'one of many' to receive a 'Dear John'. This was the expression used, regardless of the name of the recipient, to describe the letter from a girl friend, or even a wife in some cases, to say that she could see no future in continuing a relationship with no end in sight, and had in fact found someone else who was nearer and dearer. These letters were understandable in a way, when 'out of sight, out of mind' overrode 'absence makes the heart grow fonder', when it is realised that the recipients of these letters had been parted from their loved ones for anything up to three years or more, and it has to be admitted that it takes a strong willed girl to wait that long with an uncertain future in view. After all, especially in wartime, there is no guarantee that the boyfriend/husband can return.

A girlfriend/wife who can, and does wait, is a treasure worth having, hang on to her. Of course it could happen, I suppose, where the girl back home gets a 'Dear Jill' but I do not know of anyone who sent one. Although I had never actually proposed and no ring had been bought, we considered ourselves 'engaged' when I left for overseas in 1940. By 1943 I was still away and my return was nowhere in sight, so I couldn't really complain when she decided to call it a day. I heard later that she had married someone else, so maybe it worked out for the best for both of us.

After a few months at Moffat, it was decided that another Corporal and myself should go to 65 Air School at Youngsfield, near Cape Town on a Junior Armament Instructor's Course. Off we went and after a day and a night on the train we arrived at our new Station, and after settling in commenced the six week course.

This was where we were taught to polish up our instructional skills in the classroom. We had free time of course, and found Cape Town to be a large modern city, albeit with the slum areas which all cities seem to have. These were mainly older properties in what was called District Six and was inhabited mostly by the native African and

Asian population and those of mixed blood called 'coloureds'. There was plenty to do and lots of places to visit, cinemas, dances, theatres, concerts, etc. It would be a fairly expensive place to live in if one wanted to do everything. I also played hockey a few times on sports afternoons for the school team while I was there against some good local Service teams and teams from the two Universities, Cape Town and Stellenbosch. We found time to ascend Table Mountain by cable car, a real experience, the views from the cable car on the way up and from the top were quite fantastic. I went up again in 1989 and this time I had a camera.

At the end of the six weeks we had the final little exam and we both achieved a pass mark, and then it was back to Moffat and more, and I hoped, better instructing.

When we arrived back we found that there had been several changes and improvements on the station during our absence. A new entertainments officer had been appointed and a new entertainments committee formed, which was getting itself organised. The N. A. A.F.I. had been refurbished, and we were now having concerts, impromptu and pre-arranged with entertainers from the camp, and occasionally from other camps in the area, semi-professionals and enthusiastic amateurs, taking part, and doing a good job.

Best of all though was in the Corporals Club. That too had been redecorated, and the old brown lino on the floor replaced by a beautiful new blue fitted carpet, must have cost a small fortune. In addition, the club members had taken to playing the so-called child's game tiddlywinks, the carpet being an ideal playing surface. A league had been formed and on two or three nights a week, matches were played between teams of four men to a team. It must have looked quite funny to any visitors to see young and not so young men down on their knees taking this kiddies game quite seriously, and they really did. It was very popular and one good thing about it was that people didn't spill beer all over the carpet as they might have done, and did, on the lino. At the end of each league 'season', little trophies were awarded to the winning teams.

During the next few weeks I spent several weekends out in the little townships centred on the various mines, and going down the mines when invited. Selukwe, for instance was where chrome was mined, while Shabani was the source of asbestos, and gold came from the mines at Que Que and Gatooma. Coming from a mining area, but not a mining background, I was interested in these various mines and how they were worked. I managed to visit each mine and was invited to go down them and found them to be, to me, fascinating.

I also had two weeks leave in Springs, a suburb of Johannesburg. There was a gold mine there called the Daggerfontein. It was quite a large concern and the people I was staying with got me an invitation to visit it. At the time of my visit, mining was down to 7,000 feet and gosh, was it hot down there. I was told they hoped to go down to 10,000 feet before the gold might run out. The deepest mine I heard of in the area was the Robinson Deep, which was down to 14,000 feet and still drilling. I reckon that must have been hotter still.

I visited the same area again in 1989 and found the Daggerfontein had vanished. It had been worked out since I was there and even the spoil heaps had gone and the area was flat, quite a few other mines around the Jo'Burg area had suffered the same fate.

Apparently it had been discovered that although the gold had been extracted, the spoil heaps still contained uranium, not a lot but in sufficient quantities to make it worthwhile reprocessing the whole lot, so this time, instead of piling the residue up in heaps again, it was disposed of otherwise. Some may have been put back in the mine again, some might have been used for roadmaking, but whatever happened to it, it had gone, and whole areas of the landscape were flat and may make good building land one day.

Just for a change I spent one period of leave in Northern Rhodesia, in the Copper Belt, so called because of the number of copper mines there. Going there by rail, we went over the Zambezi bridge, over the river of that name, and past the Victoria Falls, a most impressive sight, 400 yards wide and 400 feet deep, and on to Livingstone, the capital. The story the local people tell, but I cannot vouch for the truth of it, was that when assembling the last girder to go into the bridge, which had been built out from both sides simultaneously, there was a five or six inch gap between the two halves. When the designer or architect, or whoever the Boss man was saw this gap, he must have thought he had made a mistake in the drawings and jumped off into the river below. This was in the early hours and the metal had contracted in the cold night air, if they had waited until mid-afternoon next day, the heat of the day would have expanded the metal again and the joint would have been perfect. Which of course they did, and it was. Anyway that is the story they used to tell. While I was in the Copper Belt, naturally I got myself an invitation to visit and go down the Rhokhana mine.

I found that the mining methods and conditions in all the mines I went down were pretty similar, but one thing I did notice was, no 'black damp' like the coal mines in England. It was most, to me, surprising to see the shift boss smoking down there.

We had only been back at Moffat a few months, when we were both sent to Youngsfield again, this time to do a Senior Armament Instructor's course. This was to be of fourteen weeks duration, and much more of interest to learn than on the J.A.I, course. As an S.A.I. I would be qualified to train Air Observers and Bomb Aimers and to do this, we had to do the complete Observers course in bombing etc. but not the navigation side of his job. In other words, we had to be able to teach and demonstrate the skills of the Bomb Aimer, both on the ground and in the air. We commenced by being given a short course on air gunnery (which we knew already, but it was part of the course) and then we did the practical side of it. We flew several sorties in an Anson Aircraft which had been fitted with a turret amidships firing twin Browning guns. We fired tracer rounds to show the trajectories of air firing, then at ground targets, and having mastered that, we went on to fire at a drogue target being towed by a Fairey Battle Aircraft. We had to do several exercises in each subject.

Then came the bombing phase. First, lectures on bombs and bomb carriers, which we also knew pretty well, methods of fusing and release, again as armourers, we were pretty well acquainted with these, but it was good to be reminded and brought up to date on the latest types. We also did a few exercises in the bombing teacher, a place we were destined to spend a lot of time in later, learning how to find wind speed and direction by the three course method. Next came the actual bombing exercises dropping 8 1/2lb practice smoke bombs from an Oxford aircraft on to ground targets on the beach. Then the same things on to sea targets from 6,000 feet. Not having the best of eyesight, I wasn't terribly good at either air gunnery or bombing, but I did just manage a pass mark. My best shot ever was releasing a bomb on to the sea target, as I thought, but it turned out to be a fishing boat, which was out of bounds on the bombing range anyway, and just missed it, fortunately. I have never seen a boat up anchor and move so quickly before or since.

We had to do test lectures on various subjects, to each other, to have our delivery and capability checked and tested by specialist officers. However, it was not all work and no play. We had hit the beginning of the hockey season again and I managed a few games with the school team, and even a couple with the Station Team. A visit into Cape Town itself was a break. Our usual place for a drink was the Del Monica which was rather interesting. The ceiling in the lounge bar looked as though it was open to the sky with pinpricks of lights representing the stars and clouds painted on it and the whole thing moved slowly across giving the impression of an open sky with cloud movement. I don't know how it was done, but it looked most realistic.

One other bit of excitement occurred one night while I was there. I was sitting on a bench by the entrance to a churchyard in one of the suburbs, talking to a young lady I knew from the camp just as it was beginning to get dark, when we heard a woman's scream followed by running footsteps behind us along a path. Without thinking, I jumped up and hared after whoever it was. It turned out to be a young man. I ran after him and he went off the path to a railing, climbed over it and fell down a bank. I vaulted over the railing and landed on top of him on the ground below. Apparently, he had snatched a young woman's handbag and run off not knowing anyone else was near. Anyway, I had winded him and grabbed him (he had broken my fall) and started to walk him to the road when a couple of policemen came running up and took over. We all went to the local police station, which happened to be close by to make statements while he was charged. I then went back to find my young lady friend and apologise for leaving her flat so suddenly, but she had obviously got fed up of waiting and had gone home. After a week or two I was summoned to appear in court as a witness when the case came up. He was found guilty and gaoled for four months.

We reached the successful conclusion of the course, and had to see the O.C. 65 Air School to be told our results individually. He told me that I had achieved a good pass, and that he was happy to inform me that my third stripe had come through and that I was now a Sergeant. Because the information had taken so long to reach me, having chased me all round the Middle East and Rhodesia, I would be entitled to eight months back pay, so I felt rich for once. I had a few days end of course leave, which I was taking when the aforementioned court case came up, and then it was back to Rhodesia once more and back to my classroom.

The people we were training were a mixed bunch, some were direct entry aircrew sent to Rhodesia for training, some were groundcrew men already out there and wanting to become aircrew, and some were chaps who were training to be pilots in Rhodesia or South Africa, but for one reason or another had failed to qualify, and were sent to Moffat to be re-trained as Air Observers or Air Gunners instead. This was normal policy.

As S.A.I.s we were allocated the task of training the Air Observers. This was quite an interesting job, teaching them what we had been learning in Cape Town. We had to start from scratch and teach them all about bombs and bomb carriers, methods of fusing and release, Pyrotechnics, and then the procedures involved to actually drop the bombs, and we hoped, accurately. This necessitated a certain amount of classroom work, followed by a number of hours in the bombing teacher, which was a three floored wooden building.

The top floor housed a machine which projected a picture through the open second floor on to a white painted ground floor. The machine could move the picture in any direction, giving the impression to anyone sitting at the side of the second floor, of being in an aircraft flying over the ground. A bombsight was mounted at one side of the second floor and there were controls to the projector to vary the picture movement, thus the operator could pick out an object in the picture, as a target, and by moving the picture, and using the bombsight, make it appear that the aircraft was heading towards the target. When the target was lined up correctly in the sights, a switch was pressed indicating bomb release. After a predetermined, which represented the time of fall of the bomb, the mechanism stopped and a small light appeared on the floor. If the sighting and all other settings had been correct, the target would be on the light.

Wind speed and direction could be incorporated in the mechanism to give the impression of drift, which had to be corrected by the operator. The slides in the projector could be of land or sea areas, thus targets could be ships or submarines, or factories, docks or airfields, in fact anything which could represent enemy territory.

Needless to say, it wasn't as easy as it appeared to begin with, but with practice, efficiency improved, though some took longer than others.

Once the bombing teacher had been mastered, the student was allowed to fly and drop practice smoke bombs on to targets set out on the ranges some distance from the camp, so the student could practice a bit of navigation to and from the range as well as bomb dropping. Sometimes a student had difficulty in getting bombs anywhere near the target and in these cases, as his instructor, I had to fly with him and watch his actions to try and see where he was going wrong and help him to correct them so as to complete the exercise successfully. This was part of the course I really enjoyed doing, especially the night time bombing.

Very occasionally we had a student who could not, or would not hit a barn door in a passage, as the saying goes. Perhaps he did not want to be aircrew and failed deliberately. In a case like this, it would have been difficult to prove and call it 'being scared', but there are people, even nowadays, who just don't like flying. Any failures we had were usually re-coursed and trained as air gunners, but once they left us we had no more interest in them. All those students who passed our part of their course, went from our side of the school to the Navigation and Radio department where they had a further period of some weeks before being awarded their flying badge or brevet, the half-wing on a large O. All were immediately promoted to the rank of Sergeant, except for two or three on each course who were commissioned.

In Rhodesia during the dry season, bush fires were not uncommon and at night, from 6,000 feet, our normal bombing height, some of these fires could be seen far and wide, sometimes a dozen or more on the ground below from horizon to horizon.

As a Sergeant, I now lived in a bunk in a wooden building near the Sgts mess. It was much more comfortable than a bunk at the end of a barrack room, and of course more privacy, but what was even more important and enjoyable was being awakened in the morning by one of the mess 'boys' with a cup of tea and a bun. That was bliss, especially when we were on early morning lectures, at 6.00am but if we were on normal start, just tea, no bun. Even that was heaven, particularly after a heavy night in the bar. I never did find out just how the 'boys' knew when we were on early or normal lectures, and they were supposed to be the inferior race.

We had dances in the mess fairly frequently, to which local people were invited, and of course our circle of friends grew and we were invited back to people's homes for leave or weekends in return. Of course at mess dances there were far fewer men, and correspondingly, more girls than at local public dances, which made dances much more enjoyable.

I was playing hockey again in the wet season. The station had a new pitch made from asbestos waste from Shabani, very finely cut asbestos and asbestos dust, laid when wet and rolled flat, which when dry, gave a beautiful hard fast surface. It was like playing on a billiard table, but woe betide you if you fell on it. Although it was hard, it seemed to have a slight springy 'give' to it.

Around that time, life seemed very pleasant indeed.

While I was at Moffat, the people I knew in Que Que gave me a cheetah skin and a python snake skin, both of which I still have. I used to keep the cheetah skin as a bedside rug in my bunk for some years until it began to show signs of wear and tear and looked a little dilapidated. It's still packed away in a cupboard somewhere in the house, in fact they both are.

I also met some people, a man and his wife, in Que Que who had emigrated to Rhodesia some years before the war. One day, in the course of conversation, it was suggested that after the war, I might like to emigrate there too. As it happened, although we exchanged letters and Christmas Cards for a year or two, we eventually lost touch and the idea never got off the ground. Actually, at one point it was a toss-up whether I went to Australia to join my uncle Hugh in Melbourne, or Rhodesia, but what with one thing and another, I didn't go to either place.

However, as always happens all good things come to an end, as did my tour in Rhodesia. I had been away from home for nearly five years and I guess I had almost forgotten what it looked like. I suppose the powers that be probably thought it was time I went back to England. It was timed very well as it happened. I had just finished a course, the students were now trained and had moved on and I was free in a manner of speaking, so I packed my kit, said farewell to my classroom and my fellow instructors, and goodbye to the people I had known on and off the camp that I had grown to like over the two and a half years I was at Moffat. Around the end of

March 1945, together with several other people from Moffat, also 'time ex' as the expression went, we entrained at Gwelo station for Buluwayo for the train to Cape Town. This would be our jumping-off point for the UK as it were.

Having arrived in Cape Town again, we first bussed out to a transit camp called Retreat (rather appropriate, I thought) and joined a lot of other personnel who were going home to England. Some were like me, time ex, others were going home on medical grounds, some were aircrew who had finished their training in Southern Africa and were going back to England for postings to operational training units or squadrons. A few who had been in Southern Africa for a few years had married local girls and were taking them back with them. Some of the female passengers were wives whose husbands had preceded them home and were on their way to join them again, but all of us were looking forward to seeing somewhat battered old England again.

We hung around kicking our heels for fourteen days, or more just waiting, presumably, for our ship to come and collect us. We could leave camp every day after roll call, and go into Cape Town or its suburbs, but it was still pretty boring. One thing I did do was to renew my acquaintance, slight though it was, with 'Nuisance', a large Great Dane dog, very well known in the area.

I will not elaborate any more on that sentence other than to say I have a book on him somewhere in the house and it is well worth reading. Some of it sounds a bit far fetched, but I can vouch for the veracity of most of it, and was actually concerned with him in a minor way in one of two of his exploits. In 1989 when I was back there I went to see the site of his grave and a statue of him at Simonstown.

At last we were put on 'stand by' and the next order the following day was 'pack kit', not that I had unpacked much of mine, and then later that same day, we were taken by bus to the docks, where we boarded a ship called ANDES. Yet another pre-war passenger liner, built for and sailing mainly to South America. She was still reasonably luxurious, even though she had been converted to troop carrying. Some parts of the upper decks was still cabins, occupied by officers, female passengers and married couples. Once again I was volunteered by some mates for gun crew duties, and again, four of us with a naval rating gunner formed a crew doing the usual 4 on and 8 off routine and once more we clicked for the Sam - 12 noon and 8pm - midnight shifts. Although we all out-ranked the naval gunner, he knew a whole lot more about 6 pounders than we did so he was the boss, and there we were doing just what we had been doing on the Ille de France two and a half years earlier.

We had some young children on board as well, including babies. We left CapeTown in daylight in the late afternoon, and saw what a lot of us thought was the finest sight in the world, Table Mountain, from the back of a ship going out. Some years later, many of us, me included, would be saying that the finest sight in the world would be Table Mountain from the bow of a ship going in. Nowadays, its Table Mountain from the air and it doesn't seem the same somehow. I must admit I left with mixed feelings. I had made some good friends out there, and the thought was there that I might go back one day, perhaps for good.

The trip home was very pleasant generally, food was quite fair and plentiful. The hours we were in the gun turret were favourable to us, i.e. we were on duty when the boat drills and inspections etc went on. The weather was calm and the surface of the sea was like a mirror at times. We saw some dolphins, a flying fish or two and the odd shark. While we were still in the South Atlantic, it was hot, no, it was very hot and remained so until we had crossed the Equator by quite a distance.

We had one rather sad episode while we were still in the South Atlantic. A child, a very small baby died of heatstroke or something, and we had the first burial at sea I had witnessed. I won't go into details of the burial, it was all rather sad for everyone on board really.

Andes was like the Ille de France, sailing unaccompanied, relying on speed to keep us out of trouble. She was a fast boat, capable of about thirty knots in an emergency, we were told. We made one call on the way home, at Freetown for mail, water etc, and while we were there, we heard a rumour that a German submarine was supposedly, somewhere waiting for us, so when we left Freetown, we went back down into the South Atlantic for a while, then turned westwards almost to America and then north again up into the North Atlantic, well west of Ireland and then east again and then south and came down between Ireland and Scotland to Liverpool where we docked in the middle of the night.

Chapter 6

Back to Blighty

Next morning, we were delighted to find that we had arrived back in England at last, even if it was dull and raining and, to us, very very cold.

Later that day, having gone through the customs procedures while still on board, we picked up our kitbags and all our gear and disembarked, and entrained for Morecambe, where we were put into what would normally have been boarding houses for holiday makers, but had been commandeered by the Government for us as billets by Service personnel. There we went through the usual processes, having a medical check-up, being kitted out to the proper scale, being issued with leave passes and pay to cover the leave period, given a travel warrant to ones home town, and finally, after about three days we were able to go off on 28 days disembarkation leave.

Naturally I went home to Redworth, but I hadn't told my father I was back in England, mainly because I wasn't sure how long we would be at Morecambe, so it was a complete surprise when I turned up on the doorstep.

After the greetings and the welcome, and a few days to settle down and meet the village people again, many of whom were newcomers I'd never seen before, having left the village about eleven years previously, and I found Redworth and Heighington to be rather dull. Most of my old schoolmates were in the Forces themselves, two were prisoners-of-war, some had left the village for good and lived in another part of the country, two had been killed on Active Service, one in Germany, and one, my sister's husband in the Western Desert. I almost wished I was back in Rhodesia, but after a week or so to acclimatise, it felt so cold in England, and find my feet I went off to London for a few days, and my goodness, how quiet it was, compared with what it was like the day I left nearly five years previously.

The black-out was still in force, but the bombing raids had practically ceased. The odd VI. or Doodlebug as they were called, a self-propelled flying bomb, or V.2. a rocket propelled flying bomb came over but nowhere near where I was. London and England seemed to have changed a lot over five years. The blitz had done enormous damage to buildings in London and many other towns and cities like Coventry and Liverpool, to name but two, and the place seemed to be full of Americans. After a few days I went back to dear old undamaged Darlington (it hadn't had a bomb on it). One stray bomb, probably jettisoned from a damaged German aircraft, had fallen in a field, north of Darlington and killed a cow, or maybe it had died of fright, but that was the only casualty in the area.

Needing wheels, I bought a second-hand Morris 12 for £40. Being on ex-overseas leave, I was entitled to a month's petrol ration, so I could get about a bit. I was able to take my father to see his brother's widow, someone he had not seen for years as she lived in a little village not on a bus route. I think he was quite chuffed that his son had got a car, even if it was an oldish one. It was probably the first car in the family, and only the second one in the village. Then one day I sold it for £42 once my petrol ration had expired. Eventually my leave period was also expired, as I got my next posting which was to R.A.F. Coningsby near Boston in Lincolnshire.

This was an operational station with two squadrons of Lancasters, one of which was 83 where I was actually going. I was working in the Armament Servicing Bay, where we serviced the bomb carriers, gun turrets, guns from the turrets and as the war was still on, we had to turn to and help with the bombing-up, mainly with 1,000lb bombs, when required. We worked seven days a week of course, but had a day off about every six days, and once a month we would get a 48 hour pass. Usually I went up to London and generally stayed at the Union Jack Club near Waterloo Station. This was a club for Servicemen on leave or pass, where a bed for the night cost sixpence. We used to go to dances or to the theatre, mostly theatre. There was a scheme organised by another Services Club, the Nuffield Centre, donated by Lord Nuffield, the maker of Morris cars, and this scheme was very popular. Where a theatre, and this included most of them, if not all, in the West End had not sold all its tickets by a certain time, all unsold tickets were sent to the Nuffield Centre where they were given out free to the, usually, long queue waiting for them. One did not always get what one hoped for, but beggars can't be choosers, as it is said, and after all, every theatre is warm on a cold night, and tickets could be exchanged between friends so that one did not see the same play twice. Besides it meant that the actors always played to full houses.

After one trip to London I was returning to camp after a 48 hour pass. When I got to Peterborough, where I changed trains, all the passengers were overjoyed to find that Germany had surrendered and the war in Europe at least, was over. It had been announced while we were on the train between Kings Cross and Peterborough. It had been expected, but to find it had actually happened took a little while to sink in. When we got to it, the market square in Peterborough, and no doubt in probably every other town and city in England, Scotland and Wales, was a seething mass of people singing and dancing, many of them more than a little tipsy, but who could blame them, and everyone was happy. I couldn't join in because I had to catch another train to Boston, and another to Coningsby, and trains do not wait, even if the war was over. At least in those days they didn't. Actually, V.E. night as it became known, Victory in Europe, was to me, and probably many more, a sort of anti-climax, we seemed to have waited so long for it to happen.

However, back on camp things did not change much to begin with. The black-out had ended and after a couple of days to settle down, life on the station had to continue. From a war time intensity to a peaceful situation took a bit of getting used to. Flying still took place, but it was mainly a case of aircrew keeping their minds and bodies still active, after all, the habits of up to six years almost cannot be dropped so easily. When the aircraft were flown, they had to be serviced, but there wasn't the same urgency. After a couple of weeks or so, I was sent on a 'mines and booby traps' course being held on what used to be Doncaster Race Course. There we were taught how to detect and recognise booby traps, how to defuze and deal with them, and also how to deal with certain types of mines, all in two weeks. I got a pass mark at the end of the course, in fact we all did, but none of us were particularly happy as we thought we were destined for a posting to the Far East, the war with the Japanese still being in progress, however far removed it seemed to be. I for one did not fancy that at all, as I had just got back after nearly five years abroad. Still when one is a regular airman, one goes where one is sent and likes it, or else.

Fortunately, or otherwise, depending on one's point of view, the war against Japan did not last much longer, the Atom Bomb saw to that. So we didn't go to the Far East after all. Once VJ. (Victory in Japan) day arrived and peace was upon us, most people started to think of demobilisation. Being a regular on a nine year engagement, my time would not be up until May 1946. So we carried on in the peace. Perhaps to keep people occupied until their date of release, some flying continued. Aircraft were serviced, bombed up and flown on training flights, dropping bombs on ground targets on Heligoland, an island in the North Sea off the German coast.

Sport of any kind was encouraged as a means of occupying spare time, as there were far more men about than really necessary for the amount of work to be done. I bought another car, a 1934 Austin 10, used it for a few weeks and then sold it again for a small profit. I took up my favourite sport, hockey, again and as I was somewhat under-employed, I was given the job of organising hockey on the station. This kept me fully occupied, arranging fixtures, usually two a week, at least, organising transport for away games, selecting the teams, all male or mixed teams of six men and five ladies (WAAF), organising meals for visiting teams in the N.A.A.F.I., at home games, putting Kit in for laundering after games and drawing clean kit for next game, in fact I worked harder than I would have done in the hanger. The team even made me captain, probably because no one else wanted the job. I tried to get a team photograph, but the only time I could get a photographer, only ten people turned out for the game, someone went sick at the last moment.

There was plenty of free time now, extraneous duties were a thing of the past, no more guard duties, service police did all security patrols etc. Dances in Boston or Horncastle were frequent, local pubs did good business, if one was inclined that way, and a lot were, 48 hour passes were granted freely, hobbies were encouraged, in fact station life was very free and easy for the first time in years. A victory parade was held in Lincoln with contingent from all the bomber stations in the area, and there were quite a few, and this was followed by a Thanksgiving service in Lincoln Cathedral, or should it be Minster, perhaps not.
By this time, men were leaving the Service in droves, every day another face was missing from the mess. It was getting more difficult to muster eleven players for one hockey match a week, never mind two, and my own demob, day gradually came ever closer. Thinking back, I don't think I was really looking forward to demob. I reckon I had been in too long and got used to the life. However, I was due out, the big day came at last and the procedure was simple.

Go by bus and train to R.A.F. Cardington near Bedford and there we went through a very well organised process to get us into civvy street. First we were given a thorough medical check-up, a suit of civilian clothes, including a shirt, tie, shoes, socks, a hat and a raincoat, in exchange for our uniform and webbing equipment. Gas masks and steel helmets had been handed in long ago. Then a leave pass was made out to cover the amount due, I was entitled to nearly three and a half months. I was given a week's pay, the remainder of my entitlement would be sent in the form of a bank draft to my home address. This was done, presumably to prevent the possibility of being robbed before reaching home. Lastly a railway warrant to the nearest railway station to one's home, thank you and goodbye.

First I went to Redworth, where I lazed around for a few days, then I went to London for another few days again, and then went to Glasgow, where, I had heard, second-hand cars were cheaper to buy than in England. I went to an auction sale and bought a 1936 model Vauxhall 14 in pretty good condition for its age. It had a fairly low mileage, and I drove it back to Redworth. Petrol was still rationed so I could get around the district, and it was possible to buy a few petrol coupons on the black market. I lazed around again for a few days and then I joined a newly formed branch of the ROYAL AIR FORCE ASSOCIATION in Darlington.

Our meeting place, at first was in the lounge of a local pub, but some time later we had our own club premises. I used to go to meetings once a week initially and at one meeting I met a chap, an ex Wing Commander whose father owned a large engineering works in Darlington. In the course of conversation he asked me if I had got a job yet, and when I said, no, I was still on leave, he suggested I might get one at his father's works.

I took his advice and applied to see if there were any vacancies. There were and I was offered a job in the tool room which I accepted. The pay was the same as I had been getting in the Air Force, and I quite liked it. The work was not terribly arduous, but it was rather repetitious. After a few weeks however, I began to get bored with the monotony, same old things day after day and wondered what it would be like in thirty odd years time. The prospect was not pleasing. Then one day, just before my leave period was due to expire, I had a letter from Air Ministry, asking if I would like to re-enlist and complete a pensionable engagement of 24 years, and if so I would re-join at my old rank and pay scale. This was like manna from heaven and I jumped at the chance.

Chapter 7

Re-enlisting

I gave my notice in at the works, sold the car I had bought a few weeks previously for the price I'd paid for it, and signed up for fifteen more years. Again I was sent a railway warrant and told to report to R.A.F. Burtonwood near Warrington. There together with a number of other Senior N.C.O.'s who were doing the same thing, we went through the usual procedures. We had the inevitable medical examination, then we were issued with a full set of uniform and webbing equipment (this was becoming a habit) and sat back to await our postings. When we got them, mine turned out to be R.A.F. Thornaby, near Stockton, about 20 miles from home, the nearest I had ever been.

When I arrived and had settled in, I found I was to work in the station armoury, servicing rifles and small arms, not that there were many to do. It was a pre-war station, and was the home of an Auxiliary Squadron, No. 608 which was still in the process of re-forming and consequently had no aircraft as yet. As a new man on the station, and like a few others, I was decidedly under-employed and was asked if I would like to catalogue the station library which had been neglected over the years and badly needed doing. Of course I said yet and got a job which was right up my street and would occupy my time for several weeks at least.

During this time, another new scheme was introduced into the R.A.F. This was called the Bounty Scheme and was designed to attract ex-regulars to re-join for a period of three years, for which, anyone taking up the offer would receive an immediate payment of £25 cash and a cash bounty of £25 a year for three years. It also applied to people like myself already contracted for twenty four years. We could commit ourselves to a further three years service for £25 cash and an extra £75 at the end of our twenty seven years, or we could commute the £75 and add it to our pension, giving us a twenty seven year pension which I opted for and was accepted for, so now

I had a long period of employment in front of me with little or no likelihood of being unemployed for some time to come.

Sometime just after Christmas that year, while still doing the library job, which I had nearly finished, the country suffered a very heavy blizzard. Prolonged falls of snow and hard frosts blocked roads and even railways in some places, frozen water systems, especially unprotected toilets on camps all over the country, and camps so affected had to send all, or most of their personnel home on special leave until the thaw came. I could not get to Redworth because the main road from Darlington was completely blocked. How people in private houses managed, I don't know. Oddly enough, Thornaby was not affected as badly as some places.

Just at this point I had another posting, this time to RAF Norton near Sheffield. I quickly finished the library job, and as the railway line to Sheffield happened to be open, off I went. I arrived there all right, but guess what! Norton was frozen up too, there were only three people on the camp. I stayed there one night, half frozen, and then went back to Thornaby which was still partly open. My bunk was still empty and my bed was hardly cold, so I stayed there until the thaw, and ate in the Mess or the N.A.A.F.I, which saved me having to pay for accommodation, I was warm and among friends. After the thaw, or at least when Norton could re-open I went back there to join No 64 Reserve Group Headquarters.

For a few weeks I did very little there either, (the story of my post war life) and then the whole unit moved to York where we took over Heslington Hall in the village of that name on the eastern outskirts of the city. It had been the home of No. 4 Bomber Group Headquarters but they had moved elsewhere and now it was our new home.

N.B. As a point of interest, although it has nothing to do with the narrative, Heslington Hall was the family home of Lord Deremore and as far as I know was taken over before or during the war by the Air Ministry as a Group Headquarters for a Northern Bomber Group. It remained in Air Ministry hands until becoming the centre of the new York University complex in the early 1960's.

The Hall itself housed the offices of the Group H.Q. and the officers mess. It was also the home of my armoury office and store in one of the cellars. What had been W.A.A.F. quarters in Nissen huts across the road from the Hall became airmen's quarters. About half a mile away, nearer the city was the Sgt's mess in a house which at one time had been a nursing home as part of the RETREAT, a big hospital nearby. My duties there were light too. I worked with the Group Armament Officer, a Flt.Lt. and my main job travelling around with him occasionally, inspecting Air Training Corps (A.T.C.) Squadrons in the North East and keeping them supplied with 22in. rifles and ammunition, and servicing the rifles if they needed it. The work was not heavy and spare time was abundant. York catered very well for entertainment, having several cinemas, and dance halls, two theatres, a football team (third division) and swimming baths, so one did not want for variety in one's off duty time.

It was there in York, one night at a dance in the de Grey rooms, one of the better places for dancing in York, where I met, admired, and fell in love with a beautiful young lady called Jeanne who I eventually married.

The best thing I ever did in my life. Unfortunately, about three weeks after our meeting, I was on the move again, this time to RAF Kirkham near Preston to do a conversion course from armourer to Fitter Armourer. Going from a semiskilled trade to a skilled trade, a step in the right direction for an increase in pay and promotion prospects, but a lengthy trip to and fro at the weekends I thought. The hockey season was just starting at Kirkham when I got there, and after a couple of practice games, I managed to get into the Station Team. All our weekend fixtures were away games, and I played in quite a few towns in Lancashire on Saturday afternoons, like Preston, Bolton, Wigan, Liverpool, Morecambe, Southport etc. They all had quite good teams. Some of the players we played against were County standard.

My weekend system was quite hectic. Each Friday mid-afternoon with the Instructors permission, I used to skive away from the hangar or classroom, wherever we were working, and get on the main Blackpool-Preston road and as I was in uniform, it was fairly easy to hitch-hike a lift in the direction I was going. Sometimes my first lift only got me as far as Preston, other times further on. Once I got a lift all the way to Leeds, and then found it quicker to continue by bus. Another occasion I got a lift from just outside the camp gates all the way to York, and as the driver was going on to Hull, he dropped me right outside Jeanne's house. I used to stay in my old bunk at 64 Grp, which had not been re-allocated to anyone, on Friday and Saturday nights, but on Saturday mornings I would get the train to wherever our Saturday match was being played. Then after the game back to York again by bus and/or train. Then I'd spend Sunday with Jeanne and her family and back to camp on Sunday night/Monday morning. This system continued until November 5th when we became engaged, and instead of spending Friday and Saturday nights at Garrow Hill (Sgts mess), I stayed in Jeanne's house, sleeping on the settee in the living room. During this period, Jeanne had been teaching me tatting (a form of lace making) done with a shuttle, and to pass the time on weary journeys on the train on Sunday nights, I used to get my tatting out and do some. I got some funny looks at times, but they never bothered me and it was a nice soothing hobby.

Note from Peter:

Tatting became a major hobby for both Dad and Mum. See more in the chapter on Tatting.

So the winter passed and spring came. R.A.F. Kirkham got as far as the semi-final of the R.A.F. cup competition but as the course had ended, and I was posted, I missed the last two games. I never did find out how the team fared in the semi-final or whether they won the cup or not.

At the end of course exams I was very gratified to find that I had achieved the necessary pass mark of 80% and was placed third overall in the results. This meant I kept my rank and was now a fully fledged Fitter Armourer and was posted to No. 609 Auxiliary Squadron at Yeadon near Leeds. This airfield is now much changed and is now the Leeds-Bradford Airport.

On May 22nd 1948, Jeanne and I were married in St. Lawrence Church in Hull Road, York. Although it was a dull day, weatherwise, we had a lovely wedding with my folks from Redworth, and friends from Darlington, one of whom was my best man, coming down, and a reception at a restaurant in York. Jeanne looked radiant in her wedding dress which she had made herself, of embossed satin, obtained with coupons (clothing still being rationed) generously donated by various friends, and a full length veil of real Honiton lace lent by another friend from Manchester, Dorothy Dearpark. My niece Margaret was the only bridesmaid, and she wore a dress also made by Jeanne. I was in uniform of course, in my (in R.A.F.

terms) Senior N.C.O's walking out dress, a pre-war uniform which was fairly rare at that time, and rarely worn anyway. I had to put in for permission to wear it which was granted, and in fact its use was discontinued a few years later. It was at about this point that I realised what with being a qualified hairdresser and a very competent dressmaker, what a treasure I had found, and it wasn't long before I also found out what an excellent cook she was too, even with food rationing still in force.

We went to London by train, for our honeymoon and stayed at the Cumberland Hotel (where have I heard that name before) in Edgeware Road, and went to a theatre nearly every night. I cannot remember the actual theatres now, but we saw 'Bless the Bride' (appropriate) 'Oklahoma', a Whitehall farce with Brian Rix, and one of the Crazy Gang shows. We also saw 'She Wore a Yellow Ribbon' at the Dominion cinema. We did a lot of walking round London, window shopping, and on the whole had a very pleasant week before getting the train back to York.

As there were no married Quarters at Yeadon, and rented flats and houses were hard to come by, Jeanne stayed at home to begin with and kept her job on, and I lived on camp except on my weekends off and the period of sick leave after I broke my ankle, playing hi-cock-a-lorum, a sort of glorified leap-frog, peculiar to the R.A.F. and usually played when one was 'in one's cups' as the saying goes. Actually, I hadn't had a drink that night which was probably why I broke my ankle. I still had to be on camp most of the week, and being on an Auxiliary Squadron meant working on Saturdays and Sundays and my 'weekends' were Tuesdays and Wednesdays when I went to York. After a few months we got a flat in Darlington and moved up there. It was the same house as our friend and my best man at our wedding lived in.

Darlington man's reunion
—with junior Minister

Wartime in the Western Desert being recalled at Yeadon Aerodrome, near Leeds, yesterday by former Sqdn-Ldr. A. M. Crawley, who commanded No. 73 Fighter Squadron in the campaign there, and Sergt. John Dobson of Pierremont-crescent, Darlington, an R.A.A.F. fitter-armourer, who was a fitter-armourer in No. 73 Squadron. The former squadron-leader was touring auxiliary units at Yeadon as Mr. Aidan Crawley, under-Secretary for Air. The sergeant said afterwards: "He remembered me as soon as he saw me and said he was glad to see me again. He mentioned one or two little incidents he took part in, but I don't think he would like me to talk about that. The last time I saw him was on a landing strip, just a little place, in the Western Desert in 1941. Then I was drafted to Rhodesia and he was shot down." Mr. Crawley filled in other details. "The place was Sidi Hamesh. I was very glad to see him today. He's the first man from the 73rd I've seen since the war."

Newspaper article about John Dobson and his old C.O.

While on 609 I was the Senior N.C.O. Armament on the Squadron. We were equipped with Mosquito aircraft when I first joined the squadron, then these were changed for Spitfires, and during my 2 1/2 years at Yeadon, we went several times to various stations on what we called 'practice camps' for two weeks at a time, for gunnery practice and training.

Once we went to RAF Acklington in Northumberland, next time it was RAF Thorney Island in Hampshire, and then it was to RAF Mansion in Kent, where I ripped my thumb nail clean off, playing cricket between aircraft sorties, but the nicest one of all was the camp we had at RAF Sylt, on one of the Fresian Islands in the North Sea, just off the German coast.

In the midst of all this to-ing and fro-ing, the squadron moved from Yeadon to RAF Church Fenton, back near York, and it was here that we got our first married quarter. It was a two bedroomed, end of terrace house, built pre-war, but at least it was a house, and in the usual Service manner of those days, it had no frills, just bare essentials. Downstairs, there was a living room, a kitchen and a larder. Upstairs there were two bedrooms, a bathroom and a toilet. It was coal fire heated, the fire being in the living room ,and when heating was required for cooking, the heat was directed by a flue system to the cooking range in the kitchen. So before the oven could be heated for baking etc, a damper had to be opened (in this case the damper was broken and had to be propped open by a half-brick) before lighting the fire, to allow the heat to circulate round the oven and to the pan hobs on top. This procedure was so dirty and time consuming, that we ignored it and bought a pressure cooker and an electric ring and Jeanne did all her normal cooking on that, keeping the oven for baking only and cooking the Sunday joint and Yorkshire Puddings.

The proper way to serve Yorkshire Puddings – on their own with gravy!

The two bedrooms each had a coal fireplace but we only used one once when Jeanne was ill. The kitchen and passage were tiled with red quarry tiles which had to be kept polished with red tile polish. In the kitchen was a stone sink and a wooden draining board, both so high that a wooden platform called a duckboard was needed so that Jeanne could reach them. There was a brick built copper (coal fired) in the kitchen for boiling clothes in, but we never used it. We bought an electric wash boiler and used the collapsible wringer which was part of the house was part of the house equipment. Off the kitchen was the larder with its marble shelf slab, and it was the coldest room in the house.

As the camp was about ten miles from York and buses were few and far between, and the railway station was a one and a half

miles walk away, I bought a car in York, a 1935 standard 10 just in time for Jeanne's 21st Birthday.

Note from Peter:

I have to interrupt again to talk about Dad and his love of cars. He had the skills to keep them running and naturally had a fund of stories about motoring in the 'old' days. Like going up a hill in York and his car progressively slowing down even with the accelerator flat on the floor. Suddenly there was an explosion from the rear, a huge cloud of black smoke and pieces of exhaust baffle clattering behind him and like a rocket the car surged forward as they gave an embarrassed wave to the amused onlookers. His 1935 Standard 10 actually had wooden floorboards which were showing their age. Mum remembered vividly the night they went out in the car all dressed up. It had been raining and as Dad drove through a large puddle, a large jet of water shot up between her feet on the passenger side, soaking, as she put it, her nether regions and making for a slightly uncomfortable remainder of the evening.

The squadron changed its aircraft again about this time, getting Meteors in exchange for the Spitfires, and it wasn't long before I scrounged a trip in the two-seater trainer, the Meteor 7 with the Training Officer. Doing aerobatics at 10,000 feet is quite invigorating, as we did dives, climbs, loops, rolls, in fact I cannot think of anything we didn't do. He even let me hold the controls for a while, it being dual controlled, but I don't think his hands were very far from the controls even when I held them.

The next thing of any importance to happen, I was transferred from the squadron to Station Armoury as N.C.O. in charge, on the out-going Fit. Sgt. being posted, but it didn't get me my crown as I'd hoped. However something much nicer happened. We had a baby, a bouncing boy who was born at Hazel wood Castle on December 2nd, 1951 in what was the local district maternity home, and is now a Franciscan Monastery. We named him Peter Grant and he was christened in the Station Church amid all his relatives from York and Redworth. He was a lovely baby and used to look ever so cute lying on his shawl in the back garden.

Peter with his Grandfathers and Grandmother

When Peter was about four months old, I was posted again, this time to R.A.F. Waterbeach near Cambridge, where I went back to my old love, instructing.

There were no quarters available when I got there so I had to go on a waiting list. It took about three months to get to the top of the list, but when I did, I officially took the quarter over and then hared back to Church Fenton to collect the family. We travelled down by car, heavily laden with all our possessions except the pram which we had sent on by rail, and there moved into the married quarter I had already taken over.

It was a nice modern house, one of a pair in a complex just a short distance from the main camp and the village from which the Station got its name. Cambridge itself was a pleasant place, full of students on bicycles and was easy to get to by car and park in, but Jeanne wasn't too keen on it as buses were expensive and infrequent, and it was awkward getting on and off them with a baby in arms. With the car it was all right, but Jeanne did not drive, so it was not so easy. London was within fairly easy reach, but I do not recall going there very often, if we went anywhere, it would have been Northwards.

I enjoyed being at Waterbeach, I liked my job, training young airmen to be Junior N.C.O.'s and giving refresher training to older ex Bomber Command N.C.O's in Fighter Command procedures and habits. I was playing hockey again and got my place in the Station Team.

Peter was growing up fast but was having a little trouble with asthma in his chest which was a trifle worrying. There was a Polio outbreak scare at one period but injections were readily available and the problem passed, and altogether we were quite happy there, but as a certain Scotsman put it, the best laid plans 'o mice and men etc, or words to that effect, when one is on to a good thing, something comes along and upsets it, and so it was with us, and the next thing I was on the Preliminary Warning Roll (PWR) for overseas posting.

In the meantime, I had extended my terms of service again and was now committed to age 55. When I went for the medical inspection which precedes all overseas postings, the Medical Officer said, before he would allow me to go, I had to have some varicose veins in my legs attended to, even though they were not giving me any trouble. So as soon as it could be arranged, I had to go into RAF hospital, Ely for a week or two and let the medics sort it out. Apparently they had to cut the ones in my left leg, which were the worst, and inject some sort of cement or other to block up the one in my right leg. It must have worked as I've never had any trouble since then. A few weeks later I had another inspection and this time all was well, fit A4 Gl. Again after another few weeks, my posting was Middle East Command, and that was all I was told. It could be anywhere between Malta and Aden.

Sorrowfully then, away from Waterbeach, saddened by the fact that I had to leave Peter and his Mum behind, to R.A.F. Innsworth, near Gloucester, pause there for a couple of days for everyone to arrive and then on to R.A.F. Lyneham, from where a plane load of us flew out in a Hastings aircraft to Malta where we landed to refuel machine and feed passengers, there being no such thing as 'in flight' meals in those days. Then on to Egypt to R.A.F. Fayid where we landed. From there we were taken by bus to El Hamrah which was a small transit camp and staging post, and this was where we would get our individual postings in the Command.

Chapter 8

To Suez and Cyprus

We were now in what was called 'the Canal Zone' and my posting turned out to be R.A.F. Deversoir, a Fighter Station equipped with two squadrons of Vampire aircraft, close to the Suez Canal. I went to work in the Station Armoury and Bomb Dump, something new to me as most of the stores in the dump were 3in. rockets and rocket heads.

Being near the Canal, one of the favourite pastimes was swimming in the Canal, but being an absolute novice when it came to swimming, I did not enjoy it very much except near the side, by the rocks. Some good swimmers used to swim right across to the other side and back again, but only when there were no ships passing through. Quite a lot of ships passed through each day and it was interesting watching all the different types and sizes of ships using it, especially at night when a convoy went through, all lit up, gliding by. See red photo album. The station did have a hockey pitch and team, so I had a few games of my favourite sport, even though the pitch was marked out on the end of a runway. It was dead smooth and as hard as iron.

Port Said was not too far away and was easy to get to by liberty bus. There was a good N.A.A.F.I. there in a guarded compound, and a club where one could spend leave in or just stay overnight in tented accommodation which was rather spartan, but adequate. There were a couple of reasonable cinemas in the town, plus the usual bars and dancing girls. One of the main things there though was the harbour with the huge statue of Ferdinand de Lesseps, the designer or builder of the canal overlooking it all. Each time I went there, the harbour seemed to be full of ships, freighters, ferries, and fishing boats, and on one occasion, we saw an Italian liner approaching the harbour, and on two other occasions saw an Egyptian destroyer and a French aircraft carrier still in the canal.

There must have been a large onion growing area somewhere not too far away, as there often seemed to be a lot of onion boats tied up at the quayside, and on one of the occasions when I went there, I took my camera with me.

After about four months there I had an airmail letter to tell me my father had suffered a stroke and was very ill. In all cases like this the R.A.F. is very sympathetic and generous as far as leave is concerned, and I was sent home on 28 days compassionate leave, on the first available aircraft, which happened to be next morning. I flew home via Malta and Lyneham, and went straight to Redworth to see him and found him out of hospital and poorly but stable. There wasn't a lot I could do for him, but I suppose just being there helped a little. I fixed up a bed downstairs for him in the sitting room, with an alarm signal upstairs for night use, if necessary. I also made a sort of lectern to rest his paper or a book on so that at least he could read, once he was out of bed and dressed. Other than that there wasn't a lot I could do really except generally help around. After some time at Redworth, I went down to Waterbeach where my family was still in quarters and stayed there for a few days until the end of my leave. Then it was back to Egypt again, this time in a York aircraft, a civilian version of the war time Lancaster bomber, flying from Stanstead.

Just seven weeks after my return to Deversoir, I had a telegram to say my father was in hospital again after another stroke. Once again I was given 28 days compassionate leave and flown back to England as before. Unfortunately, by the time I arrived at Redworth, he had already died on November 27, 1954. A few days later the funeral took place, and he was buried near where my mother had been buried nearly twenty years before. After helping my sister sort out certain legal details and a few other odds and ends, the family and I went back to Waterbeach, where I was able to have a family Christmas, something I hadn't thought I would have, and on New Year's Day 1955 I flew back again to Egypt.

When I arrived back at the transit camp, I found that as part of the run-down of British Forces in the Canal Zone, Deversoir had been closed and I had been posted to 109 M.U. at R.A.F. Abyad. There, I was in Station Armoury again and a lot of my time was spent working on ejection seats something comparatively new in the RAF, out there anyway, and having done a short course on them at the Martin-Baker factory, I was the only N.C.O. who knew anything about them. Away from the canal, I spent a lot of my spare time on my tatting, having embarked on the ambitious task of making a tablecloth.

One of the highlights of my period at Abyad was the visit of an E.N.S.A. concert party led by Harry Secombe. The party visited several stations in the Canal Zone, and came to Abyad and gave a show in the station cinema, after which they were entertained in the Sgts Mess. Actually I don't know who entertained who, we them, or they us, but a good time was had by all.

A few days after this, I became due for normal leave, having been overseas officially for nine months and no hope of a married quarter. Compassionate leave is always ignored in leave entitlement reckoning, therefore I was entitled to twenty one days leave and a free flight home. So there I was on a flight in a York back to UK and who should be fellow passengers but the concert party who had concluded their Middle East tour. When we landed at Malta for food and fuel, sharing our table was Harry Secombe himself. He's a real character, both on and off the stage. He was chatting away to us all through our meal, asking about my family, if any, and I showed him a picture of Peter on his tricycle in our garden at Waterbeach and he asked if I minded if he autographed it. Naturally I didn't mind and he then said would I like him to get the other members of the party to sign as well, and I said I would, and he did.

After this trip, a nostalgic twenty days in England, during which we had a week's holiday at Butlins holiday camp at Clacton,

Winner of The Knobbly Knees Contest at Butlins

where we had a lovely time and the end of my leave seemed to come far too soon, and I was off again back to Abyad, but only for a short period this time. Suddenly, I was given a gang of blokes and sent off at short notice to R.A.F. Nicosia in Cyprus, just a short trip in a Viking aircraft, a civilianised Wellington bomber. Having arrived at Nicosia and bedded down, as it were, I was told my task. The Air Publications and Forms Store contents were being transferred from the Canal Zone to Cyprus, and our job was to receive it, erect a large marquee to store it in, under cover, pending the erection of a permanent building. We had to sort it all out as it came in, tons of Forms and more Forms, Air Publications, posters, books of every kind. It looked as though it would take months.

During all this, we were classed as part of the Station and subject to Station discipline, which meant taking part in the monthly Saturday morning parades, and on one of these parades, another Sergeant and myself were the star turn, in a manner of speaking. The parade formed up, was inspected and then we were called out to the front where we were presented with our Long Service and Good Conduct medals. These were for eighteen years unsullied service, or as said before, earlier in this narrative, undetected crime. Another ribbon to sew on one's tunic.

Just after this episode, I got my actual posting on the Island. It was to Akrotiri, a new airfield on a peninsula at the south of the Island, and meant that my detachment was now a posting and I could have my family out there with me, so I promptly had them called forward with the idea that by the time they arrived I would have completed my current assignment, and that was just how things worked out.

Akrotiri was a new station in the course of construction and I was one of the first thirty or so personnel posted in. There were no quarters as yet, so I had to get down to Limassol, the nearest town and was lucky to find a small bungalow to let, which I rented, so we had somewhere to live. I had to hire furniture as well, as there was none in it. My job with the Forms Store was nearing its end and as it happened, its conclusion coincided with the arrival of Jeanne and Peter. I had hired a car and met them at the airport, and away we went the fifty four miles to Limassol. I had arranged a couple of days leave with Akrotiri to give me time to settle in, and we installed ourselves in the bungalow and settled down to a new style of living. Jeanne had never been abroad before, so it was all new to her, and of course Peter was all excited by it.

Our landlady lived in a village up in the mountains in the Platres area and we paid the rent into her account in the bank every month. The bungalow was, I suppose, fairly typical of Middle Eastern architecture, flat roofed and consisting of a hall/living room, dining room, two bedrooms and a passage with toilet and bathroom off, leading to the kitchen which had a stone sink in it and for cooking, a 3 burner paraffin stove with an oven on top, which could be removed and pans used on it. The bathroom was most interesting as far as water heating was concerned. The heater consisted of a metal cylinder of water which was heated by a hollow 5 inch diameter pipe up through the middle, with a fire of wood or paper or anything combustible at the bottom. The pipe was also the chimney and it was surprising how efficient it was. All the windows were shuttered.

One very funny thing happened the second morning we were there. A knock at the door, Jeanne opened the door and without even a good morning, a man walked in carrying a pack on his back and a syringe of some sort in his hand, and went down the passage to the toilet, squirted some liquid into the loo, then into the bathroom, did the same thing in the wash basin and bath, then into the kitchen and repeated the action into the sink, turned round and before leaving, reached up and took a card we hadn't noticed from the back of the door, wrote something on it and left, just like that, not a word spoken. It turned out that he was a council hygiene man doing his weekly anti-malarial visit.

We settled down quite well and Jeanne started to get to know the neighbours. As they were all either Turkish or Greek, language was a bit of a difficulty, but she managed. We were the first English people in our little area, so she had to. I went to work with four other people, also comparatively new arrivals, in a taxi, laid on by the camp, as there were no buses out to Akrotiri, to take living-out personnel to and from camp. The fact that one of the five was an officer might have had some influence there. Later as the numbers increased, a bus was laid on instead, in fact when I left to return home two years later the station strength had grown and including civilians, more than a dozen buses were needed to transport all the people in and out.

The total strength was under 40 when I first got there, but every day seemed to bring more and more people in. I was the first armourer and obviously the first N.C.O. and my armoury was a cupboard in the guardroom but things changed rapidly over the next few weeks. I went from a cupboard to a whole room and then to a lockable trailer, and then as 103 M.U. was forming as buildings were completed, I had my own section, and a Station Armoury was completed and had its own N.C.O. staff. Meanwhile, off the camp things were changing. Just before Christmas a Greek policemen was killed by what became known as EOKA terrorists, a Greek Cypriot organisation, fostered by Greece, it was claimed, demanding union with Greece, which started, to say the least of it, a period of political unrest.

It wasn't very long before the unrest became what almost amounted to open warfare. It became Island wide and quite a few British soldiers and some airmen were shot, always from behind, and others killed in bombing incidents of various kinds. We had two incidents on the camp, in one, a tin of aircraft dope with a few sticks of dynamite taped round it was placed by a hangar door, but before it exploded, it was found safely defused. The other was different and backfired on the would-be assassin. He was riding a motorcycle with a bomb inside his saddle bag when apparently it went off just after he had passed the Sgts mess. All that was found afterwards was a lot of mangled metal and not much of the rider. It must have contained quite a lot of explosives. Even in Limassol itself there was a fair amount of trouble, some, just a crowd of schoolchildren chanting 'Enosis, Enosis' which I believe was Greek for unity or freedom or something. Sometimes there were large demonstrations by thousands with the same object in view. Moving about in Limassol was not at all safe at times. Service children went to school in buses with wire netting over the windows and an armed guard on each bus. People like myself, living off the camp, were detailed to patrol the streets in the vicinity of our houses, accompanied by two Turkish special constables for different periods in the evening before midnight. Luckily the only thing near us was the planting of a petrol bomb under the car of a friend of ours who lived a few yards down the road, which didn't explode.

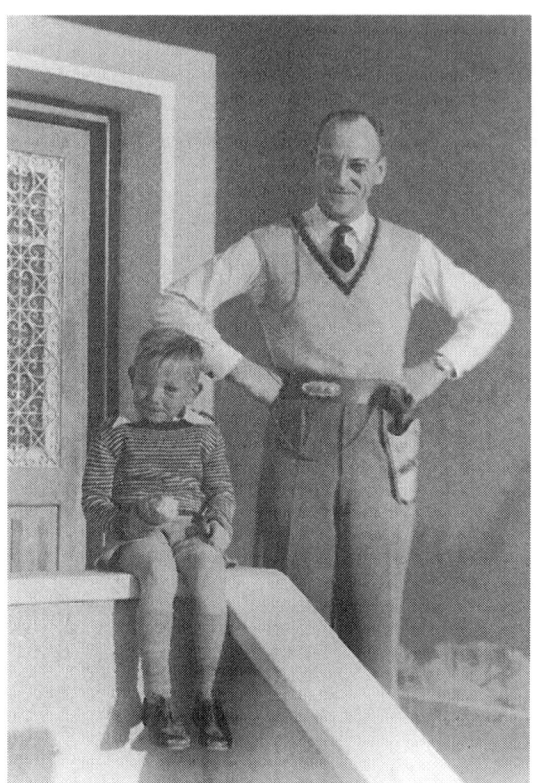

John using Peter's Roy Rogers holster for his service weapon as it was
more comfortable and efficient than the RAF issued one

Every now and then a curfew was declared, when no one was
allowed to enter town, or even leave their houses in some places.
At times, English people were advised not to go into town. Some of the
main streets were barricaded with barbed wire, with gaps in the barricades
guarded by British soldiers, and Servicemen were banned from going into
town at all at these times. If, and when we did go out, we had to be
armed. Imagine us walking down St. Andrews Street (one of the main
shopping streets) me leading the way holding Peter's right hand in my left
hand, leaving my right had free to get at the gun I had to wear, and
Jeanne walking behind me to make sure I couldn't be shot in the
back. It became our normal method of progress, and in fact it
became such a habit, that later when we were back in England and in
transit at Blackpool, every time we left the house, Jeanne automatically
fell in behind me, until she realised what she was doing.

Periodically, aircraft from Nicosia used to fly over dropping propaganda leaflets, and Peter used to join the Greek kids picking them up by the handful and we used to put them into the bathroom heater. We still have some of them in a Scrapbook Jeanne kept up while we were out there.

The second November 5th that we had out there, the army decided that, EOKA or not the British were determined to celebrate 'bonfire night'. The Army Camp at Polemedhia was the venue. A large bonfire was built on the football pitch, and personnel and families from the Limassol area received invitations to attend and were brought in by buses. The football area was ringed by armed soldiers facing outwards to deter the unwanted and a grand night ensued, with bonfire, fireworks, hot dogs and coffee all supplied by the Army, all for the benefit of the kids, young and old in the area.

One good thing about living where we did was the fact that there was a small Turkish market just passed the end of our street, and the Turks being anti-Greek ignored curfews and opened as usual. It was mainly fruit and vegetables and meat, so we could always get food. In front of the market there were always a couple of lambs or goats tethered and we used to say they were reserves.

The next item of importance was when Jeanne found she was going to have another baby so we were all agog. She carried on as usual for a while and then found the house work was too much really, especially in the summer heat, and she could do with some help. So she got a Turkish lady to come in and give her a hand. Her name was Nedimae, if that is the right spelling. She was a widow with a son called Ali and must have been a devout Moslem as she used to read the Koran every day at 4 o'clock. They lived in the street just behind us. At first our little street had no name, then one day a council official came round with a list of names and asked the English ladies in the street which one they would prefer and they chose an English name, Alexander Fleming Street and it stayed that way, and the last time we were out there on holiday some years later, it still remained so.

In 1956 we got an increase in overseas living-out allowance. It was back dated a few months, so we used the extra money to go towards buying a car. We bought a new Fiat 600, a new model just being introduced on the island.

It was small but big enough for us, and the situation being what it was, we could not go far in it except to Ladies Mile.

This was a long stretch of beach along one side of the peninsula where the sand was clean and soft and shelved so gently into the water, one could walk out over 200 yards and the water was still only half way up one's thighs. It was ideal for young children and there was no tide. The only problem was, if there was an off-shore breeze, and a blown-up air bed was being used to lie on the water, it was essential to tie a rope to it and to a stake in the sand to prevent it being blown out to sea, as one nearly was one day.

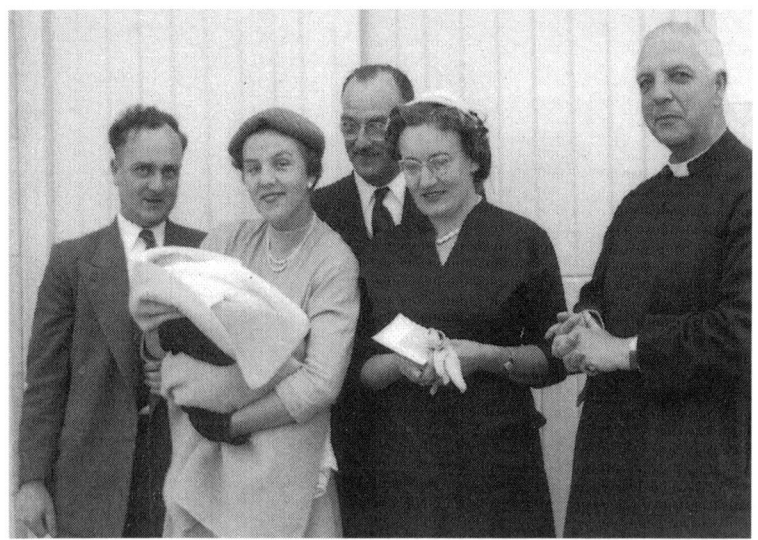

Attending the Christening of the child of friends and neighbours.

142

Another occurrence, if that is the right word to describe it was what became known as the Suez Crisis. It had a lot of publicity at the time, national and international. I won't go into the whys and wherefores of the trouble, but for a short time we were heavily involved at Akrotiri. I had been busy for quite a while starting up a new section in 103 M.U. for the maintenance of small arms, and larger up to 20 m.m. guns, bombcarriers etc. Bofor guns were already being serviced in the bay next to mine, but when the Suez trouble erupted, I locked up my section and reported to the Station Armoury, where I was given a Cpl. and five men and we went into the area of scrubland we laughingly called the bomb dump, no security, no fences, just stacks of rockets, rocket heads and a few bombs

There we started on rocket preparation. Our task was to unbox the 3 in. rockets, test them, fit fins and rocket heads, load them on to bomb trolleys, and deliver them to the squadrons which had newly arrived. We had Vampire, Venom and Hunter squadrons to cater for, and believe me, we were kept busy, and I think, only lost one aircraft, a Vampire, and pilot. There were also two French squadrons on the Base, but they had their own armourers and equipment etc and we were not concerned with them at all. Fortunately the crisis did not last long and when it was all over, I went back to my section and continued ordering stocks of tools and spares.

At the beginning of the Autumn term before he was five, we had Peter started at school. We thought he was ready for school and after I had seen the Station Padre who was also the Education Officer, he agreed, so Peter got into the routine of going to school while we were still abroad.

He seemed so grown up with his water bottle hung round his neck going off with his mum to the end of our street to catch the Service bus with its armed guard, to take the children from the immediate area to the school which was in fact, a bungalow on the other side of the town.

Just before Christmas, 1956 our second son was born at Polemedhia medical reception centre, which also served as a maternity unit, on the outskirts of Limassol. Like Peter he was a lovely baby.

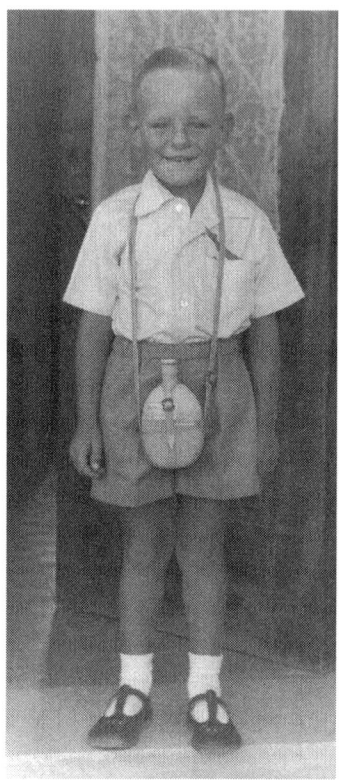

Peter's first day at school

Although I could not go every day to see him, it was not considered wise to establish a regular habit, for obvious reasons, I did go occasionally and took Peter with me, even though he was not allowed to enter the ward. One Sunday night, just after I had left, there was a very loud explosion not far away from the hospital area. All the ladies in the wards were afraid one or more of the visiting husbands might have been involved. As it happened, no one was, the explosion had been well away from the road we were on. At last I was able to bring both mother and baby home and we were a united and bigger family once more.

When the time came to have him baptised, the ceremony took place at the camp church, and to get there we had two little Fiats into which we managed to pack thirteen persons, adults and children. However, we arrived and unloaded amid much amusement among some onlookers as person after person emerged from the cars. The station church was newly erected and Roger

John, as he was named was the first baby to have the honour of being christened there. A baby girl born to parents from the station was the first camp baby, but she was christened in the original camp church which was a large tent in, what would be the married quarters area when the quarters were completed.

Roger and Peter

Political trouble continued on the island until Easter 1957, when E.O.K.A. agreed to a truce, which meant we could get around in the car, visiting all the places we hadn't been able to go before. Places like Nicosia, Paphos with its lovely little harbour and the Pelican Restaurant, Famagusta, a walled town with a deep water harbour and docks, and an imposing building which had alternated being a cathedral or a mosque for centuries, Larnaca, with the ruins at Salamis, and the tomb of Uum Haram believed to be a relative (aunt) of the prophet Mohammed, who fell from her mule, died and was buried at that spot. It is known as the Tekke and is considered to be a holy place and Turkish ships dip their flags when they pass by at sea. We also went of see St. Hilarion Castle in the northern part of the island, which, we were told, was the backdrop for the film, snow White and the Seven Dwarfs.

On Easter Sunday we went to the top of Mount Olympus, the highest point on the island, with snow still on the ground under the trees, where we had a picnic. Cyprus is a delightful place full of happy memories. We have been back there on holiday several times in the last few years and met again some of the people we knew before. It is a great pity that the island has been split in two, both physically and politically.

In June my three year overseas tour ended and we were posted home. Before we left I took the car down to the docks, had it put on a lighter and taken out to the ship that was bringing us home to Liverpool. Both Peter and I also went out on the lighter as well to see the car hoisted aboard and secured, and then had a ride back to shore. We were finally taken to Nicosia airport, having duly handed the house and furniture back to the owners, and flew back home to Stanstead in a Skymaster aircraft.

Chapter 9

Back in England

From there it was by train to Blackpool, where all families went on disembarkation in England, into a boarding house normally used by holiday makers, to await a posting and spend their disembarkation leave there if they wished. As soon as I was told of its arrival. I went to Liverpool to collect the car. Now we were mobile and after a few visits here and there to see relatives and show off the new baby, I took up my new posting to R.A.F. Waddington near Lincoln where I went leaving the family in Blackpool until I was allocated a married quarter. As it turned out, it did not take too long, but long enough for both children to have chicken-pox, one after the other. Jeanne did not enjoy her stay in Blackpool at all.

At last everyone was fit again and I went up to Blackpool in the car to collect them and once more we were united again at 6 Vulcan Street, Waddington, Lines, to give the full address. My first job was N.C.O. i/c in the Station Armoury. On the arrival of a Flt/Sgt to take over, I moved from there to 83 squadron as N.C.O. i/c. A Flight Armament, being concerned with bombing-up practices, loading panniers for trips overseas, ejection seats, and so on. After a couple of years there, I checked with Records Office and found that I had slipped back a few places on the promotion roster, and I could see no progress in the way of promotion to Flt. Sgt., so the other way was the Technician Ladder, and anyway the pay was the same, so I went on a refresher course to R.A.F. Melksham in Wiltshire, took and passed the exam, and became a Chief Technician, the equivalent of a Flt. Sgt. in pay but supposedly superior in technical ability.

As a result of this, I left the squadron and took over the post of instructor in the Bomber Command Vulcan Servicing School, newly vacant owing to the previous incumbent being commissioned, a post I was to hold for seven years, the first three at Waddington. During those three years we relaxed and enjoyed ourselves.

Not much fear of being whipped off overseas at short notice, no squadron exercises to worry about, and we went everywhere in our little Fiat. We joined the Fiat Car Club, based in Lincoln, and in this club we took part in rallies, treasure hunts, navigation exercises, day an night, and had an annual show and exhibition, where in the latter I won the concours d'elegance three years running.

We used to go to Stapleford Woods in the spring to see the magnificent displays of rhododendrons each year and to Clumber Park in the Sherwood Forest in the summer to picnic and play cricket with the boys when fine.

Peter was in the Cubs and doing very well with an armful of badges. He played the recorder quite well, and with another boy got their entertainers badge doing an impersonation of Nina and Frederick by having a record played behind a curtain, and them miming on the stage in front of the curtain.

Then with the family growing bigger, in size not numbers, and the Fiat seeming to be getting smaller, I sold it for almost what I paid for it, five years previously, and went to the other extreme and bought an Austin A70. A big black monster with a 2 1/4 litre engine, 5 years old but in good condition and it suited us down to the ground.

During this time Peter had completed his primary school education and had been offered a place at North Hykenham Grammar School, and Roger was just about to begin his proper schooling after the camp nursery school. However, both boys had to change their tactics, as B.C.V.S.S. moved lock, stock and barrel at short notice, to R.A.F. Finningley near Doncaster, so Peter started his secondary education at Thorne Grammar School, and Roger started at the camp school. We had gone into married quarters at Finningley not long after I got there, but after a few months we thought we should be putting some roots down and decided to buy a house in Thorne. It was better for schooling for both boys, no bus to catch and although it was a reasonable walk to school, the exercise was good for them.

The house we bought was in Kirton lane on the outskirts of Thorne and was fairly old, 1929 vintage and needed a bit of renovation which I did myself or had done professionally, such as some electrical wiring which looked a bit 'dodgy'. It had a small lawned garden at the front and a small stream outside the front hedge. At the back of the house was a yard with an outside toilet, a coalhouse and a big outhouse which had been used as a bakery at one time and was now the wash house. There was a large wooden garage and behind that a lawned area with fruit trees in it, and then a large vegetable plot which unfortunately was pretty solid clay which took a lot of digging but produced some good potatoes. The house had three bedrooms and a bathroom etc, upstairs, and two rooms and a small kitchen downstairs. Altogether nice and compact. No central heating of course.

As it was ten miles to Finningley, the Austin was a bit costly to run to get to and from work, so I bought a little motor cycle, a Honda 50, a hundred miles to the gallon and about 35 m.p.h. It was very nice in dry or sunny weather, but not so good when it was raining, which it often was, especially in the winter. After about a couple of years there, I had trouble with the Austin, which although not really serious, would have been expensive to put right, so instead, I traded it in, in part exchange for a Mini. Not a good move as it turned out. By the time I had used it for a year, all the front end was more fibreglass than metal, and a good part of the doors and body. However, it didn't matter a great deal. We had now been at Finningley, or rather I had, for four years and I felt that my time at B.C.V.S.S. must be running out. During this time Peter had completed secondary school education and gained a fistful of 'O' Levels. Sure enough, one day the Orderly Room .rang up to tell me that my screening in my present

post had been withdrawn and that I was on P.W.R again for overseas service.

I was given a choice of areas (most unusual) Cyprus, Germany or Singapore, in that order. I opted for Singapore, never having been in the Far East before, and was highly delighted to get my first choice and the station was to be Tengah. How things had changed in ten years, at one time, one was posted to an area or Command, and to a station on arrival in the Command. There were no problems with the medical exam, this time, and it wasn't long before I had my actual leaving date. Fortunately, I had just finished a course and no successor had been mentioned so I had no one to hand over to, however, that was not my problem. I had a few days leave before I left during which I sold the Mini and the motor bike.

I had to leave the family behind in Thorne, until I could be allocated married quarters which I hoped would not be too long, although it might take Jeanne a while to sell the house before she and the boys left. As things turned out, on the Sunday morning before I was due to leave, I put a notice in the front garden, 'House for Sale', Sunday afternoon some people came to see round it, and on Monday afternoon, not long after I had left for Stanstead, they came round again to say they would buy it. So that was one problem Jeanne would not have to worry about when her turn came to leave.

Chapter 10

Off to Singapore

I flew out with fifty or sixty others in a Britannia aircraft, one of those old fashioned ones with four fans at the front. It was a long and rather boring trip. The first stop was Istanbul which took about five and a half hours to reach, much of it in the dark. The aircraft was refuelled, the passengers had a meal, and we sat around the airport for well over an hour and then with a new crew aboard took off again just before sunrise. The next leg was even worse, it took over nine and a half hours to get to our next port of call, Bombay, about 17.00 hours. I thought Egypt was a smelly place to begin with, but when we walked down the aircraft steps at Bombay, the heat and the stench, and that was the only word for it, hit us like a brick wall. Again a meal and refuel, and by this time the smell wasn't so noticeable, and off we went again with a new crew on the last leg. By this time I felt so weary, I think I slept most of the way and only woke up when we landed at Paya Lebar Airport, Singapore, about three o'clock in the morning, local time, another seven hour flight. We disembarked and cleared local Customs with very little trouble, if any, and a bus took us to R.A.F. Tengah, about ten miles from the airport. I checked in at the Sgts mess, found a bunk had been reserved for me, stripped off, as it was already feeling hot, pulled a sheet over me and slept like a log until well after lunch. Then I got up, had a shower and then went to the Orderly Room and arrived officially.

Next day I reported to Tech. Wing H.Q. and was directed to the Armament Squadron which was split up into four sections or sites. I was assigned to IX site which was the Bomb Dump (a large one) where the man I was replacing was due to return to UK in a couple of weeks or so. A Warrant Officer was in charge, and I would be his second dickey with the title of controller. We had quite a large staff including a sub-section which serviced bomb trolleys. After a couple of weeks getting acclimatised and used to the job, I was settling in nicely and just waiting for the family to arrive. This they duly did, and by the same route that I had taken. I met them at the airport, at the same unearthly hour, and we were taken to a rest house where we would stay until I got a quarter.

Eventually, I was allocated one and we moved into a nice airy house in Hunter Hill, the nicest quarter I have ever seen. It was one of a pair in a road of similar houses in the camp married quarters area, just a short distance from the main camp. It was nicely furnished with rattan (cane or bamboo) chairs in the living room which had a carpet over tiles, and wide doors opening on to a front verandah leading to the front garden and front door. All the floors, upstairs as well, were tiled which meant it was fairly cool. There were three bedrooms, a toilet and bathroom with a shower (an absolute necessity) upstairs, and downstairs, a living room, already mentioned, a dining room, a kitchen and at the end of the house, the amah's room with toilet and shower and a sort of rear hall or scullery opening on to the rear garden.

All the rooms had ceiling fans, as far as I remember, and the main bedroom also had an air conditioner. We had an amah, or maid and I got an extra allowance to pay her with. She was a great help until Jeanne was fully acclimatised, then at the first Christmas, when we could have done with her most, she had or took ten days off for public holidays, of which Singapore had many, having umpteen different religions on the island. Having done her own housework for those ten days, she thought she might as well continue, so the amah was dispensed with, and Jeanne managed quite well without her. A good job we were a tidy family.

We also had a garden 'boy' who came round once a week to cut the lawns and looked after the flower beds for which we paid him a small sum per month. As well as our garden, he looked after quite a few other gardens too, so it was worth his while and ours. He even used to bring and plant a couple of pineapple plants in the garden which, in time, grew to be nice big pineapples. The front garden had a covered pathway, built by some previous occupant, leading to the front door. This was rather pretty and had several different creepers like honeysuckles and bougainvillaea growing along it and by the front door was a banana plant which produced small bananas in season. Once a week, in the early evening, workers from the Station hygiene section came round the quarters, spraying the hedges, front, side and rear with some sort of anti-malarial liquid. Whatever it was, it obviously worked as Singapore was classed as being malaria-free.

Shortly after our arrival in Singapore, I bought a 1956 Wolsley 1500, an excellent car, and not a spot of rust anywhere. We kept it for the full three years we were there and went all over the place in it, clocking up about 40,000 miles in it in those three years. We went up into Malaya on leave on at least three occasions, once into the Cameron Highlands, a popular area for leave to escape the heat of Singapore, being anything up to 7,000 feet above sea level. On the way there we visited Malacca and spent the first night in a Government Rest House, and then on to Kuala Lumpur where we lunched at the Station Hotel and then after some sightseeing carried on to another Rest House at Tapah for the night. We continued next day past the Robinson Falls where there were myriads of butterflies of all colours and sizes, some six inches across the wing span, to Ringlet where we had hired a bungalow for a fortnight.

The climate at that altitude is lovely, around 70 degrees F. and there are some excellent jungle walks, some man-made, and some natural in varying degrees of severity. We also visited a tea

Cameron Highlands

Note from Peter:
*   We stopped so I could photograph the water buffalo shown above and Dad walked with me. I stopped a good distance away but Dad said we'd be fine going closer, "Just like the cows on the farm, they won't bother us". We went closer and I took the photo – just before the one with the big horns put its head down and charged. We ran.*

plantation and saw the tea being picked, and then all the stages of drying, sorting and eventually packing, some in packets, but mostly into chests for export. There is a restaurant/hotel built in mock Tudor style called Fosters Smoke House not far from Ringlet where they serve the most delicious steaks and strawberries, but not together of course.

Note from Peter:

The roads in the Cameron Highlands were steep and twisty. The exit from one hairpin bend was so steep that the Wolsley couldn't get up it, even in 1ˢᵗ gear and the bend was too sharp to build up enough speed. Dad simply told us all to get out, turned the car round and reversed around the bend and up the steep section where we re-joined him. That desert mountain convoy experience had taught him a few tricks – "cars have more torque in reverse gear", he said.

Travelling through the back streets of Singapore City

Another time we went to Port Dickson for two weeks, again a very nice seaside town with docks as well as beaches, and on a third occasion to Malacca itself for a few days. We frequently went to Jason's Bay on the east coast of Malaya, a long sandy beach of dark, almost black sand stretching for around 9-10 miles in a huge curve, a very popular spot.

Walking out on the beach with Peter and Roger

One of my Sgts and several of his mates used to go somewhere on the east coast of Malaya at weekends on diving trips and during their dives they used to bring up shells of all kinds. I bought some of the shells they brought back to help defray some of their expenses. One was a 'Horned Helmet' which I still have together with several others. They had a rather strange way of cleaning out the insides of the shells. They buried them in the ground, left them there for 4 - 5 weeks and let the ants do the rest. When the shells were dug up they were as clean as a whistle apart from a bit of soil which easily washed off.

Singapore city itself and the Island as a whole had a feast of places and things to see and visit, like the Botanical Gardens, Crocodile Farm, the Cathedral, the House of Jade, Change Alley, and a host of others too numerous to mention. Of course I must not forget the Kranji War Cemetery and the Johore Zoo. Before I leave the places to visit I must relate the story of one of our trips to Johore.

One day we decided to go to Kukup on the south west corner of Johore. This village was a tourist attraction, being built out over the sea on stilts. It was a fishing village originally, but because of its position, it was cashing in on its tourism interest. We went out in a boat for a trip around the bay, viewing the houses from the water.

Even the temple was above the water. It had a restaurant whose speciality, naturally, was sea food. One thing that amused us was the toilet in the restaurant. It was used by both sexes and consisted of a square wooden cubicle with a bolt on the inside of the door. It had a concrete floor with a hole in the middle. It had no chain to pull, but the sea was directly below and the tide did the rest. There were wooded islands off shore and a police launch continually on hand on the look-out for smugglers. On the way back from Kukup we noticed heaps of pineapples by the roadside, just like the piles of turnips or sugar beet we see by the roadside in England in autumn. I suppose they were there waiting to be picked up and taken to the canneries.

On the camp itself, there was plenty going on too, especially as far as we were concerned in the Sgts mess. Every Friday night we had a darts league. I was in a team called 'the Vagrants', who won several competitions and I still have some of the trophies. Most Saturday nights, there was a musical evening with a 'group' and perhaps some cabaret acts from town followed by music for dancing, but Jeanne and I were not into modern dancing, and now and then there would be a filmshow, but not often.

On special occasions such as Christmas, New Years Eve, Midsummer or any other time the mess committee decided was worthy of the occasion, there would be a special Ball and these were really splendid occasions.

Ladies wore long dresses and the men correct mess dress, short white jacket and white shirt with black bow tie, blue cummerbund and miniature medals were the order of the day or rather night.

A glass of punch was offered on arrival at the mess and a corsage of flowers for each lady. Partway through the evening a pause to give the band a break, a sumptuous supper was provided for the guests and mess members by the catering staff, and they really were meals to be remembered. We used to be invited to other messes on the island too, perhaps to Seletar or Changi or an Army or Naval mess. One New Years Eve we had been invited to the Ball at Nee Soon, a Naval and Marines mess. It had been raining almost nonstop for a few days but we got there all right, and on the way home after a very pleasant evening, about three o'clock in the morning we found that one side of the dual carriage-way was blocked by sand washed off the hillside, and we had to drive all the way back to the Tengah turn off on the wrong side of the road. Luckily, at that time of night, we met no oncoming traffic.

Another occasion at Nee Soon to which Jeanne and I were invited was the presentation of new colours to 42 Commando, Royal Marines by H.R.H. Prince Philip. We had been given a special invitation by a friend we had originally met at the rest house on our arrival in Singapore, who was a W.O. in the Marines and he was to be escort to the colour in the parade.

Again it was best bib and tucker for the guests as there was to be a reception afterwards. The parade and presentation was a most impressive sight, especially as it was an evening ceremony and seeing the column of marching men as they approached the parade ground from a distance, in their white helmets was an unforgettable sight.

Christmas was always a special period, one of the highlights being the Christmas bars. Most sections would build a bar in the section, and this would depend on the size of the section as to the theme chosen. I cannot remember them all over the years, but I will mention a few. One was a replica of a Wild West Saloon, another, a South Sea Island scene, another was like a French Cafe, another in the R.A.F. Regiment hangar depicted a jungle scene, yet another was based on the T.V. prehistoric series, the Flintstones. Those are just a few of the many. It was amazing what could be done with some paper, paint, plywood, a lot of ingenuity and hard work.

For weeks before Christmas, it seemed that all the Hercules aircraft staging through Gan brought dozens of crates of English beer on every trip. This of course was for the bars and was sold at cut price rates. The idea was, I think, to discourage airmen from going into Singapore at Christmas, getting drunk and possibly into trouble, and who would if the beer was cheaper nearer home. A day or so before Christmas, the Station Commander went round to judge the bars and award prizes for the best three in order of merit, and then each night up to Christmas and maybe even the New Year, the bars were open for the sale of beverages or whatever and a jolly good trade they did, any profit going towards next year's bars.

Eating Satay at a mackan stall in Tengah village

One of the Hindu festivals celebrated every year in February, I think was Thaipusan, a very colourful occasion. I will try and explain what it looked like but I have some slides which show it much better. There was a parade of hundreds of Hindus who walked all

163

the way down Orchard Road to a temple in the city, I forget its name now. All these people carried a Kavadis, I think it was called. This was a decorated wooden frame carried on the shoulders. They, the males were bare to the waist. There were men, women and even children in the parade or march, whatever it was called. Attached to chests, upper arms and shoulders by hooks into the skin were limes and other things. They also had silvers of wood (skewers) through their noses, and some had similar things through their cheeks and tongue. Other things were attached to their legs as well. The strange thing was that where the skin was pierced, there was no blood, not even where the tongue was skewered. After the walk one year, we watched them at the temple having all these things removed and even then not a drop of blood from any of the removal points appeared, and then the priest or whatever doing the removing, seemed to touch the places from where something had been removed with a touch of wood ash, or so it seemed. We were told later that those parading were put into a trance so they would feel no pain during the decorating or the walk. It is difficult to describe but one can only say what one saw, but I must admit it was a trifle weird.

Another thing that stands out in my memory also occurred at Christmas, or rather just before it. Roger was at the camp school, and they were having the usual fancy dress party prior to going off on the Christmas holidays.

Jeanne had made a special dress and hat etc. and with white shoes and socks, dressed him up as the fairy that fell off the Christmas tree, complete with twisted wand. I took him to the school in the back of the Landrover I used at mealtimes, and what a howl of laughter went up when he got out at the school entrance. Needless to say he won first prize.

What else can I remember about our life in Singapore?. Yes, snake stories. We had a snake as a pet for a while. One of the chaps I worked with was very keen on wild life, a naturalist, I suppose he would be called. Most weekends he would be out in the jungle, either on the island or over in the Johore ferreting around to see what he could see or find. One Monday morning he brought a Chinese rat snake into my office and said would I like it. Having recovered from the surprise I accepted it (he assured me it was quite harmless) and took it home where I made a cage for him, or her, from a large three-ply wooden box with a glass front and we kept it on the verandah. We would let him out in the living room at night where he would roam around and eventually curl up under the rattan settee. It was said that any house with a snake in it would never have burglars. We never had any. Incidently we called him Cedric, Goodness knows why. Unfortunately, after some months he/it died from some unknown cause or ailment.

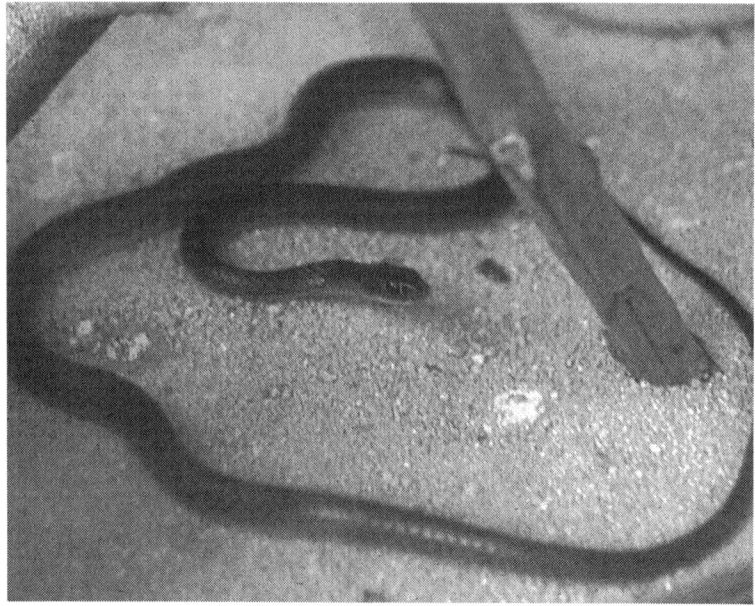

Cedric the snake

Some time later, we had a visitor in the rear porch one night, another snake just over a foot long, much smaller than Cedric. I didn't know what breed it was, so put a cardboard box over it and next day sent for the Corporal in the Hygiene section who also knew about snakes, who came and took it away. Apparently, it was a Kukri, again harmless but I don't know what he did with it.

166

My next snake story is Peter's really as he was concerned with it. While he was in Singapore he took up 22 in. small bore rifle shooting, it being less strenuous than rugger or soccer and became rather good at it. He joined the small bore club at Tengah and shot in matches around the island, and on several occasions represented the Far East Air Force Team and won a number of little trophies. On one shoot he was firing in a competition at 100 yards when the Range Officer called out for all except Peter to stop firing. He then told Peter there was a snake near his target and to hit it if he could. Peter could and did, and it turned out to be a cobra, jolly good shooting by any standards.

The Rifle Range

Another occasion when Peter got mixed up with a snake might have had serious consequences. He was with a school party in Malaya and one day spotted a small snake in the grass (no pun intended) or somewhere when they were on a nature walk of some kind, and quickly put a glass jar over it. Somehow or other he managed to get the snake into the jar and the lid on. When it was shown to the teacher, he went white and nearly had a fit, and told Peter to be careful and not drop the jar. What the final outcome was, I'm not sure but apparently it was one of the three most poisonous snakes in Malaya.

Peter was also concerned in another incident involving a snake (seems to make a habit of it). A friend of his, also living in quarters, had bought a python in the village of Nee Soon. A wire cage had been prepared and off they went to collect it. At the Nee Soon shop, or wherever it was kept they went to a long box about as big as a freezer, and as Peter put it, when the lid was opened, all they could

167

see were coils of python. With difficulty, they and the vendor managed to stuff it coil by coil into a sack. They carried it to a bus stop and got on a bus. The bus driver asked what was in the bag, as the contents were moving, and when they said snake, the bus stopped with a lurch and they were bundled off. After two attempts at getting a taxi, but as soon as snake was mentioned as the contents of the sack, the taxi hared off. At the third taxi when the question on the contents of the sack came up, they said rabbits and had no trouble, and got it home and caged. The python measured about 12 ft. in length and broke out of its cage the next night and escaped back to jungle. One or two of the younger boys in quarters had pythons for varying lengths of time and used to show off, wearing them around their necks like scarves.

74 Squadron Lightning at sunset – The Flying Blowtorch!

Another 'snake incident' which did not concern any of us personally for once, but hit the headlines in the local paper. I had a phone call from Air Traffic Control to say a snake was heading across the runway in our direction, IX site being on the other side of the runway from A.T.C., and what was I going to do about it. I do not remember what I said, but I was told that my reply was to the effect that there wasn't much I could do about it except shut the door. Later on that day, a Lightning from 74 Sqdn was landing and at the end of his run, when slowing right down to turn off the runway on the taxiway, a 14 foot python wrapped itself around the nose wheel leg. "The photo shows the pilots of 74 holding the snake.

One totally different 'incident' was when Roger and a friend were standing on a footbridge over the Bukit Timah road chewing gum and spitting off the bridge on to the road. A Chinese gentleman who nearly got an 'eyeful' naturally objected to this habit and complained to a policeman who promptly 'arrested them'. We then had to go and rescue them in a manner of speaking, after profuse apologies to the gentleman concerned and a promise to never do it again. The Chinese do not take kindly to being spat upon. Can't say that I blame them and had words with young Roger on the subject.

I had one interesting day out once after we had reports that some of the rocket heads fired into the ranges at Asahan, up country in Malaya, had failed to explode. These had to be checked out and dealt with where necessary. A twin Pioneer aircraft from Seletar with a Sgt. bomb disposal expert and two helpers came to Tengah for me and one of my Cpls. and we all flew up to the jungle landing strip near the ranges, at 1,000 feet all the way. Being low, it was a slightly bumpy ride but I enjoyed the trip. The B.D. Sgt and one of his men were almost green but not actually sick, and soon recovered after we landed. We did a bit of digging and searched the area pretty thoroughly, but only found one unexploded head which the Sgt. soon dealt with using a slab of guncotton and a one ounce primer and detonator. When it came to leaving, early in the afternoon, the aircrew could not get one of the engines started, so a radio call to Seletar for help which arrived in another aircraft. The fault was rectified and the aircraft left.

We then started up and prepared to leave too. At this point, some heavy guns, which had been silent since our arrival, opened up on the ranges and the shells were whistling overhead at intervals. Our pilot got in touch with the Army by radio and explained the position. The army gave us five minutes to get off and away, and I don't mind admitting that I hoped they didn't hurry to start again as we were not off for at least ten minutes, and I'm sure I heard one shell whistle over before we left. It was a very short runway and I wondered whether we would make it, but the pilot heaved back on the stick at the last moment and we lifted off just over the treetops.

In Singapore and Malaya, no doubt due to the climatic conditions, there was a profusion of fruit, soft fruit mainly. In Malaya, in the Cameron Highlands, as mentioned previously, Strawberries were the thing to gorge on, big, red, juicy and sweet, just beautiful. There were other things too of course, but those stand out most in ones memory. In Singapore itself, there were many fruits of different kinds, again mostly soft fruits, they probably grew just as well in Malaya, but we were not there long enough on leave periods and visits to sample all on offer. Pineapples grew in both places like turnips do in England, in fields, but I have already mentioned that. Rambutans were very popular too, a large gooseberry sized, red coloured fruit with a rough skin but beautiful to eat when peeled, also good for canning. Then there were bananas which seemed to grow everywhere, including our front garden. Another one I recall was called Durian, a very peculiar plant. The fruit was large coconut sized with soft flesh under a thick skin. It smelled awful, but get past the smell, the fruit was delicious, or so I was told, I could never get past the smell. My favourite was mango, about five inches long and again thick skinned. Mere words cannot describe the taste, it was out of this world. I thought so anyway. We used to eat them for breakfast, see slides again, but I always used to say, the proper place to eat them was in the bath, they were so juicy. I think that is enough about fruit, oddly enough, many of them are available in England now, either raw or in cans.

Mangos for breakfast

One thing I must not forget to mention, Roger will never forgive me if I do, and that was his school speech day. After some time at the camp school, he- passed the MacMullen (I think I've got that right) test which was the Forces children's equivalent of the 11 plus, and he with about 600 others in the area went to one of two schools, some distance apart, but classed as one school and run by the army, I believe. Roger went to the one called Bourne. The other was called Gilman. At the end of the second year, the two forms of that year had a combined speech day held in the Singapore National Theatre. It was the only place with a stage big enough to accommodate all the children involved, and an auditorium large enough to seat all the family members attending the ceremony. It was quite an impressive occasion with all the children on the stage, and the various dignitaries from each school. First there were the speeches, as always, then singing by school choirs and finally, the prize giving, of which Roger was one of the recipients.

My tour should have lasted two and a half years, but Peter was in the middle of his 'A' level course, so I applied to have my tour extended to three years so that he could finish it, and we liked being in Singapore anyway. This was agreed but I had to give up my quarter and move into private accommodation. This proved to be comparatively simple and easy. I found a chap who was going home at the same time as I should have done, who was already living in and about to vacate a bungalow in Jurong, a suburb of Singapore and not too far from the camp, and as I had the car there were no transport problems, so a quick chat with him and his landlord, and I could take over his place the day he moved out.

About a month or so before the move took place, I had a nice little job given me. I was literally detailed to organise the Guy Fawkes day bonfire and firework display. This was usually done by the Armament Section in UK, while we had been in Singapore there hadn't been one. Perhaps they had enough fireworks at the Chinese New Year celebrations. As this was likely to be the last year of British influence (I won't use the word occupation) the Station Commander, at one of his weekly meetings of Senior Officers, decreed that there should be one and the order passed down office after office till the buck finally stopped with me.

As I hadn't bought any fireworks for a few years, I needed help, so I chose two of my youngest armourers, both still in their teens and asked them if they would like to help choose the fireworks as I hardly knew what to get. They jumped at the chance of a day off and armed with a thousand dollars, Singapore, (about £150) from a Station fund, we took the Landrover and went shopping in the city, and they, in fact all three of us thoroughly enjoyed ourselves.

In the meantime, a large bonfire was being built in an open space in the camp. The day, or rather night arrived, the fire was roped off to prevent children getting too near too soon. The proceedings opened with the firing of a star shell and the fire was lit by the Station Commander as custom demands. It was a grand display, even though I say so myself. We tried to work it so that something was happening, either going up or coming down, all the time with no long gaps between each item and it concluded with the traditional illuminated GOOD NIGHT.

Apparently, everyone enjoyed it, and the Armament Squadron had a congratulatory paragraph in Station Routine orders next day.

A couple of weeks or so later we moved house. The new one was nice and clean so we had no problems in moving in, much cleaner than some we had moved into. The only snag was it poured with rain all day and the next day. We soon settled in and took stock of the surroundings. In addition to the house I even took his dog over as well. A lot of private dwellings in Singapore were surrounded by a 54-60 inch wire mesh fencing, as a deterrent against thievery which was pretty rife off the camp, and a dog was a useful deterrent too especially if it was a good house dog and Jock as he was called was all that.

Sunbathing with Jock

He was a mongrel of mixed ancestry but he was a grand dog and would fight and win any dog twice his size, in fact he was king of our area without a doubt, and accepted me master right from the beginning.

We had Chinese neighbours on one side and an Australian army W. O. on the other, and opposite was a Japanese family. Also in the street, which was called Jalan Layang-Layang, were three or four American families whose husbands worked in the oilfields in Java or Sumatra or somewhere like that, so we were quite a mixed bunch nationally. We stayed there very comfortably and were still able to get around and go places. Peter finished his course and I completed my three years. By this time, the British Forces in Singapore and Malaya were being run down rapidly and things were changing, so I think we left about the right time and at the end of the three years I sold my car to a New Zealander, handed the bungalow over to a new tenant, and Jock to one of the Americans who wanted him (and used to feed him steak when he escaped to do his rounds, he ate better than we did!) We then moved bag and baggage back to England after what would be my last overseas tour. We came back the easy way, by jet, a V.C.10, first leg to Gan, an island in the Indian Ocean where the R.A.F. had a base. The usual meal and refuel, a walk round the camp to stretch our legs, and then off again to the next stop, AKROTIRI in Cyprus.

There we left the aircraft and stayed in Cyprus for a pre-arranged holiday for a week, which we found had not changed a great deal, at least in the south anyway, which no doubt Peter and Roger will tell you all about.

Revisiting Ladies Mile beach 13 years later

Note from Peter:

We had a great time in Cyprus as Mum and Dad took us on a guided tour of the island's many attractions. We were staying in hotel in part of Limassol called Heroes Square and me being anxious to check out the "action" in the area, set off on my own that evening. The first bar I walked by had an attractive girl stood outside it who gave me a big beaming smile and asked me to buy her a drink. I politely declined and said "perhaps on the way back", thinking to myself "Wow she fancies me!" but also being acutely aware that my pocket money might not stretch to a round of drinks at unknown prices and perhaps I should hare back to the hotel and scrounge some money from Dad. I continued my walk only to find another gorgeous female outside the next bar, also asking me to buy her a drink. I gave her the same reply but I was pretty chuffed to find myself so attractive to the local girls. As I passed the third bar and the same thing happened again, it suddenly struck me that the girls were actually prostitutes. Suitably chastened, I went back to the hotel and at dinner in the hotel I described my encounters.

Mum spluttered over her drink and said, "That explains a lot. I was sat in the lobby and a man offered to buy me a drink, when I said my husband would be joining me soon, he gave me a funny look and walked away. You know what John, the RAF have only gone and booked us a hotel in the ruddy red light district!"

The highlight of the holiday was revisiting the house we used to live in and being recognized with much fuss and celebration. The main family that Mum and Dad had known well insisted we have a meal with them that night which turned out to be a huge party as word had been passed to all the old friends and relatives that had known us.

Then a week later back to Akrotiri for the last leg home in a Britannia again. After our return from Singapore we went into the Blackpool area yet again, but instead of going into a boarding house as we had done on previous home-comings, we got a temporary quarter in a partly occupied housing complex at R.A.F. Warton, and settled down for a while.

Chapter 11

Back in Blighty again

Peter got himself a job as a barman in a nearby pub to keep him occupied while he waited to go to University, having secured a place at Swansea. School holidays had started in England so Roger was at a bit of a loose end. I wanted a car and having driven one on hire during our week in Cyprus, decided on a VW Beetle. I could buy one through N.A.A.F.I. and get 10% discount, but the only garage operating the scheme that I could find was at Croydon. So I ordered one by telephone, specifying a red 1500 c.c. engined model and when it was ready, went up to London to collect it. Having taken possession, mid-afternoon Saturday, I drove back up a motorway, the new Ml for the first time. It had not been open very long and had very little traffic on it. I was 'running in' so did not exceed 40 mph, and from what I saw nothing was going very fast at all. What a difference now, road crowded and most drivers doing 80-90+.

However, I got back safely, and now that we were mobile, the first place we went to was York. We couldn't stay with Jeanne's mum and Don as there was insufficient room at 38 for an extra 3 people, so we hired a caravan on a nearby site and used that for sleeping. We also paid a visit to Redworth to see my sister and brother in law and other relations in the area, and then it was back to Warton again, awaiting my posting, which wasn't very long in being sent to me - it was to R.A.F. Coltishall near North Walsham in Norfolk, after asking for a posting to North Yorkshire before I left Singapore. Typical of R.A.F. Records Office.

Still, Coltishall it was, and I found my new job as Controller in the Missile Servicing Section working on a Red tops and Bloodhounds a lot different from being Controller in a bomb dump. School holidays were nearly over and no sign of a quarter yet, so to get Roger into his new school at the beginning of term, I had to get him down to North Walsham and board him with a man and his wife, a very pleasant older couple, for a few weeks until I was allocated a quarter. He went to Paston School, which everyone knows, or should, in the school's view, was Nelson's old school. For a while then, Roger went to School and I went to work. Some nights I went to see him, some nights he was doing homework, or I was on duty, but at the weekend we would be into the car and to go Warton, however this did not go on for long as I was eventually allocated a quarter, had our furniture which had been in store in Doncaster, sent down and with Jeanne down from Warton we were a family once more. Peter was at University so he was out of the way, in a manner of speaking.

We settled down to our normal quiet existence and Jeanne started thinking about getting a little job, preferably clerical, and making use of her 5 'O' levels she had gained in Singapore. At this point we were also thinking again about house buying and had settled on a plot in North Walsham and having a bungalow built on it, when suddenly it was all change again. I got the opportunity I had wanted, a posting to North Yorkshire which would be my last tour of duty, presumably. It was to R.A.F. Leeming, about twelve miles up the road from Dishforth, where it had all started in 1937.

The builder quite understood and made no bones about cancelling our tentative house building arrangements, after all, nothing had been signed and he had other customers in the pipeline. Then I was soon on my way again, leaving my family behind once more, they must have been used to it by now.

I arrived at Leeming, and having booked in and settled in, found I was to be working in the Station Armoury as N.C.O. i/c ejection seat servicing bay, a job very much to my liking. Having looked around for a day or two, I discovered it was 14 miles to Northallerton and as I didn't fancy living in quarters on the Station, I cast about for an alternative temporary arrangement until we could get the house we wanted. Then someone suggested I try for a Council house as he didn't think there was a very long waiting list. I took his advice and applied for one, and in a few days was offered a brand-new never been lived in council house.

This would be the stop-gap until the bungalow we had long planned could be built or bought. Then I discovered that this could be much nearer than we had dreamed of. I found out that the local

Council had an area of land which had been marked out into plots and these were being sold, not to a developer, but to individuals who could buy one, and after the normal planning application had been granted, could build on it, in fact had to build on it within three years or lose the plot. I could hardly believe our luck. I went to see the Town Clerk, and was shown the plans of the area. I picked out one unsold site which I thought Jeanne would like and my name was pencilled in on the plan. I was over the moon.

I was still living in the mess of course, but every night for a week or more was down at the council house, scrubbing and cleaning so that it was fit to live in. Then I arranged to have the electricity and gas turned on at the mains and then went down to Coltishall to give Jeanne the good news. She was delighted and came back with me next day to see what lay ahead. I showed her the plot, but horror of horrors, she didn't like it, it was North facing, something I had not thought about. However, all was not lost and we went back to the Town Clerk and lo and behold there was a South facing plot on the other side of the road and a hundred and fifty yards nearer to the town not spoken for. He immediately changed my name from one to the other, and we were back to square one again. Meanwhile, or rather, eventually Roger's school term ended for the summer holidays and he left permanently. I took a couple of days leave, booked the furniture removal van and we left Coltishall with all our belongings and no regrets and moved up to Northallerton and into the council house.

Once we had settled down, a friend of my niece (our bridesmaid) a draughtsman by trade drew up the plans from a sketch I had given him. These went with the planning application to the Town Council offices, and after a while planning permission was granted, and then came the hard work. I had been given the names of two bricklayers who had just finished a house and were free to take mine on. They were very good and helped me a lot. First they put me in touch with other tradesmen such as, a carpenter, plumber, electrician and a tiler for the roof. I agreed that these blokes be called in as required. They also did their own quality surveying and ordering of bricks, sand and cement etc. All I had to do was to pay the bills, and I knew I wasn't being 'rooked'. From remarks I heard later, they were honest men. Sometime after the house was finished and we were living in it, someone asked me who had built my house, and when I told them, they said I need have no worries about it, they are the two best 'brickies' in Northallerton. A remark like that gives one a very pleasant feeling. All this time we lived in the council house quite comfortably and at weekends we did labouring work on the house, in fact, I reckon, between us Jeanne and I handled every brick used, in moving them from one place to another and then somewhere else as required.

While this was going on, I continued to travel daily to Leeming and work in the ejection seat bay, a most satisfying job, especially as on one occasion on a training flight the aircraft got into difficulties and both the student and the instructor had to bail out. They both ejected and landed safely while the aircraft ploughed into a field not far away. The Station was a training station equipped with Jet Provosts, so with two seats per aircraft I had plenty of work to do, even with two very efficient assistants, a Sgt and a J/T to work with.

In the meantime Jeanne had got a job in the local Rating Office, thus putting her five 'O' levels to very good use, mentally and financially.

After the construction work on the bungalow was finished we did the decorating ourselves and saved a packet on that. Then came the big day when we moved in having had the carpets laid and the furniture moved professionally, and now we had something we could really call our own, except for the Mortgage, which, as I'm writing this much later, we cleared some years ago, and it is a wonderful feeling to be able to think and say, we don't owe anybody a penny. Our only regret now is that we didn't build it just a little bit bigger, but we hadn't thought of grandchildren then.

After some months I began to realise that the time was not too. far away when I would be leaving the Service. Therefore instead of continuing to my actual retirement date, and the possibility of not finding another job, plus the fact that I hated the thought of having to 'go on the dole', the very thought of that was abhorrent to me, I decided to try and get a job before I left the R.A.F. and as I fancied clerical work, I wrote to the Civil Service, but they didn't have the decency to reply, perhaps my letter found its way into the laugh and tear up tray, or maybe I used the wrong form.

Then I saw an advertisement in our local paper, the Northern Echo, saying clerks were required at County Hall. I applied for a post, and was invited to attend for an interview. I attended, was interviewed, offered a post in the Education Department and accepted it all in the same afternoon. Next day, I gave notice of my intention to terminate my service, which had previously been agreed should my job search be successful. A month later, after the normal period of notice, I left Leeming for the last time on Friday night and started work at County Hall on Monday morning.

My first position was in the room in the Education Department where we calculated the pay and allowances for all school employees, teachers, cooks and kitchen workers, schools meals supervisors, caretakers and cleaners, groundsmen etc. After working with one of the other clerks, and being shown the ropes, as it were, it being something entirely new to me, I soon found my feet and it became quite interesting. Over the next two years I learned a lot about things like enhanced overtime payments, maternity pay and leave, sickness pay and sick leave, groundsmen's and cleaner's bonuses, which always struck me, I must admit as a means of getting more money for less work. The only thing we didn't do, I believe, was the calculation of income tax which was done by the County Treasurers Department.

As a result of Local Government reorganisation in 1974, I gained some advancement in position and consequently salary increase, but as usual my feet were itching again (the story of my life) and on seeing, in an internal bulletin, a notice of a vacancy for a 'SENIOR ESTABLISHMENTS CLERK' in the County Fire Brigade, I applied for the post. To my delight I was invited to go to the Fire Brigade Headquarters for an interview with the Establishments Officer, the Chief Administrative Officer and the Chief Fire Officer, all the top brass I thought. The interview was obviously satisfactory as -later that afternoon I was very pleased to be informed by telephone that I had been successful and the appointment would be confirmed in writing as soon as possible.

I became in effect, the Salaries and Wages Officer for the whole of the North Yorkshire Fire Brigade, Wholetime firemen and Officers, Retained firemen and Officers, Control operators and all civilian staff, dealing with pay and allowances, sick pay, leave, retained firemen's bounties, maternity leave for female staff, in fact preparing payrolls for onward transmission to the County Treasurer's Department at County Hall.

I continued in this post for nine years or thereabouts, the longest I have ever been in one place continually, and the longest I have ever been in one actual job until I had to retire finally on my 65th birthday. Thus I went from 14 years of age on leaving school to 65 and was never actually out of work, a pretty fair record with which I am reasonably well satisfied.

Post Script

Most of the time I was at Leeming and before the house building started Jeanne had been busily engaged in the Valuation Office, not rating as I called it before, she was actively engaged in the last valuation of properties that took place in 1971/2 . Then the valuation office in Northallerton closed, with the work being transferred to Harrogate or Darlington. She did not want to travel to either place, so transferred as a C.O. to the D.H.S.S. in Northallerton for quite a while only fortified by the fact that the salary she earned was bolstering our bank balance. The job itself was rather soul destroying but she stuck to it. She had several spells of Acting-up to E.G. the last one being most of her last year of service which helped her pension. In 1983, she and several others were offered the opportunity to retire early and draw their pensions and lump sum immediately instead of waiting to age 60.

As this coincided with my retirement date, she accepted it and retired on December 31st, 1983, just before my own retirement in January 1984.

We then settled down, not to a life of indolence, but trying to do a lot of things we had not been able to do before. We decided we would try and have two holidays a year, Spring and Autumn and try to go to a lot of places we would like to see, abroad if possible, and this we did. In between times we visited our two sons, one in Wales and one in London.

We have five wonderful grandchildren, Peter and Nerina have two, Miranda and Marcus, while Roger and Mary have three, Sam, Milly and Max, and we have a lovely relationship with both families.

Fortunately, our health has remained, on the whole, good. We walk a lot, two-three miles a day (into town and back again) or more occasionally, in fact we both feel fitter than we did when we retired.

Chapter 12

Tatting

This article published in The Daily Mirror in 1960 reads:

"The judges didn't hesitate for a second when they saw the intricately designed tablecloth in a national arts and crafts competition.

"Exquisite!" they said and awarded it first prize in the embroidery class. But then had a shock.

They discovered the cloth had been made by – A MAN !

"It took me a year to do," said Sergeant John Dobson, 41, a R.A.F. armaments fitter, yesterday. "I reckon I worked on it for about 600 hours in my spare time".

Tatting.

Sergeant Dobson, stationed at Melksham, Wilts, made the cloth in tatting.

"This is done with a shuttle and a crochet hook is used to link up the stitches into a design.

The competition was organised for the Forces by the YMCA at
Tidworth, Hants.
Sergeant Dobson beat women entrants from all three services.
"The cloth is an absolutely exquisite example of tatting", said Mr. D.M.
Smith, Principal of Southampton Art College and one of the judges.
Now it is on show to the public among the 400 other exhibits at
Tidworth's YMCA centre from 2 pm to 9 pm

Tatting whiled away his time on train journeys

SIXTEEN years ago Chief Technician John Dobson, at present stationed at R.A.F. Finningley, used to watch his girl friend—now wife Jeanne—happy with her handicraft hobby of tatting. Before long he too became an enthusiast and used his newly-acquired art to pass the time on long train journeys to and from business.

Today he is an expert and recently won first prize in the national Royal Air Force Hobbies and Handicrafts Exhibition in London.

MANY AWARDS

His exhibit, a 3ft. 6in. square table cloth, was made during the last three years in off duty hours from his post of armaments instructor. His wife, a hairdresser, also sent off entries and gained a " highly commended."

The couple who live in Kirton Lane, Thorne, have made many dressing-table sets, table cloths, handkerchief edgings, and so on. They hope eventually to pass on their knowledge of tatting . . . tatting is said to date back more than 400 years . . . to their 13 years old son, a pupil at Thorne Grammar School.

Having once become a dab hand with the tatting shuttle Chief Tech. Dobson, started to enter his work in many local and national shows gaining many awards. He has not only exhibited in this country but also during overseas tours. He has competed directly against the ladies by entering and gaining a third in a competition organised by a national women's magazine, and he also gained a " highly commended " in a national contest at Earl's Court.

In a year he usually completes one big tatting job and 12 smaller articles. For an armaments instructor he has certainly chosen a hobby with a difference.

10/12/64

JOHN DOBSON

This article published in another national newspaper in 1964 reads:
"Sixteen years ago Chief Technician John Dobson, at present in R.A.F. Finningley, used to watch his girlfriend – now his wife Jeanne – happy with her hobby of tatting. Before long he too became an enthusiast and used his newly-acquired art to pass the time on long train journeys to and from business.

Today he is an expert and recently won first prize in the Royal Air Force Hobbies and Handicrafts Exhibition in London.

MANY AWARDS

His exhibit, a 3ft. 6 in. square table cloth, was made during the last three years in off duty hours from his post of armaments instructor. His wife, a hairdresser, also sent of entries and gained a "Highly´ Commended".

The couple who live in Kirton Lane, Thorne, have made many dressing-table sets, table cloths, handkerchief edgings and so on. They hope eventually to pass on their knowledge of tatting...tatting is said to date back more than 400 years...to their 13 year old son, a pupil at Thorne Grammar School.

Having once become a dab hand with the tatting shuttle Chief Tech Dobson, started to enter more work in many local and national shows gaining many awards. He has not only exhibited in this country but also during overseas tours. He has competed directly against the ladies by entering and gaining a third in a competition organised by a national women's magazine, and he also gained a "highly commended" in a national contest at Earl's Court.

In a year he usually completes one big tatting job and 12 smaller articles. For an armaments instructor he has certainly chosen a hobby with a difference.

Northern NOTEBOOK — The pages abou...

SATURDAY, JULY 13, 1991 · Your contact: JUNE HAWDON, Darlington & Stockton Ti...

Hooked by an age-old art can make a chap better for all tat

This article was published in The Darlington and Stockton Times in 1991 and reads:

WHILE fellow airmen were downing their pints, Sgt. John Dobson had a different pursuit.

After becoming hooked on the art of tatting Saturday evenings in the mess were never the same.

Mr Dobson, of Turker Lane, Northaller-ton, was inspired to tell how he became interested in tatting after reading our recent Notebook article on Mrs Pamela Stredwick and the Cleveland branch of the Ring of Tatters.

He and his wife are also members of that branch and his interest in the ancient art goes back to Mr Dobson's courting days when the farmer's son, whose family originates from Melsonby, was stationed at York.

It was back in 1947 that he met his wife-to-be, Jeanne, an accomplished tatter. When he was moved to the Preston area, she taught him the hobby to help pass time on long train journeys

At first he turned out yards and yards of tatting which was used to edge pillow cases but soon went on to bigger and better things. He became an outworker for Coats-Patons, checking that patterns sent to them

190

actually worked - and often they didn't, he says.

In fact, the firm bought the rights to one of Mr Dobson's own patterns for the princely sum of £25, he recalls.

He and his wife both enjoy the relaxation of tatting and although Mr Dobson hasn't actually overtaken his wife as far as achievement goes, she admits he has tackled much bigger projects. Among these is a beautifully-worked cloth in very fine 40-gauge cotton which he entered in an R.A.F. competition, beating all entries including those from WRAFs. And he went on to win lots more prizes, including medals through Woman's Own and craft prizes at Heighington Show when his family lived in Redworth, near Darlington.

Mr Dobson even took his tatting with him when he was stationed in Egypt. Travelling light, his work tools are all contained inside an old spectacles case, though he hopes one day to find a Victorian or early 1950s shuttle to add to this.

"I got rather bored out there and that's where I started the big cloth," said Mr Dobson, who reckons he spent around 1,000 hours on this work.

"While the others were drinking, I was tatting," he said. Nothing new to the 73-year-old who, while stationed at Yeadon, tatted between pulling pints on bar duty in the mess.

His wife learned to tat from a West Yorkshire woman, surreptitiously watching her at work as she was keen to guard her secret, being the only woman in the area able to do it. She was highly delighted that her husband picked it up and said: "He's really dedicated and gets down to it."

Among his achievements was a unique luncheon set comprising 19 mats of varying sizes, which he worked as a wedding present for American friends. Their delight on receiving the present will never be forgotten by the Dobsons, who hope that one day one of their four grandchildren might also take up the hobby.

Mr Dobson, who spent almost 36 years in the R.A.F., finishing up at Leeming, said tatting is a hobby he enjoys immensely, no matter how small the item he is working on. These have included tiny butterflies which he was commissioned to make for the owner of an Oxford craft shop, who used them as a trademark on personalised stationery.

Last Christmas Mr Dobson elaborated on this idea, making festive decorations for his own cards. "Just for a handful of special people," he said.

Tools of the trade

15956924R00102

Made in the USA
Charleston, SC
28 November 2012